RAF NATIONAL SERVICE
IN SIX MOVEMENTS

First edition / revision 2
published in 2006 by

WOODFIELD PUBLISHING
Bognor Regis, West Sussex, England
www.woodfieldpublishing.com

ISBN 1-873203-98-5

Cover photo:

Truleigh Hill 1957.
Back: John Shefford, Tony Stirling, 'Doc' Kinsey,
Front: John Glover, Roy Taylor.

RAF National Service in Six Movements

Cardington ~ West Kirby ~ Sandwich
St. Margaret's ~ Barkway ~ Truleigh Hill

ROY TAYLOR

Woodfield

For Joyce

Contents

Preface

Medmenham lies on the North bank of the River Thames, just inside the Buckinghamshire border, midway between Marlow and Henley-on-Thames. Only the river separates it from Berkshire, while the borders of Oxfordshire are a few miles to the west. I am tempted to wonder how many people outside of these three counties are aware of its existence.

Walkers on this splendid stretch of the Thames footpath will know all about Medmenham. Their guidebooks will tell them how Sir Francis Dashwood leased Medmenham Abbey in the mid-eighteenth century as a base for his notorious Hellfire Club. In his excellent book, *The English River,* Alan Titchmarsh reports that Satanic rites were enacted in the shrubbery and that the gentry cavorted around in monk's habits, chasing scantily clad nymphettes through the Abbey ruins. Titchmarsh typically adds the comment 'Tut-tut'.

The name will also strike a chord in the memories of a large number of service personnel who served at RAF Medmenham during its existence from pre-war to the 1980s

I have recently walked this section of the river, but my first awareness of Medmenham came 45 years earlier as a young just demobbed National-Serviceman in the blue uniform of Her Majesty's Royal Air Force. I can still remember the cold January morning when, in the company of Sheff and Harry Harris, I emerged from the café by the crossroads to catch the bus into Marlow and from there to pick up the threads of real life that had been put on hold two years earlier.

Sheff, or John Shefford to be precise, had been with me for most of the two years and Harry had crossed our path on a couple of occasions at radar courses at St. Margaret's Bay and Barkway, but none of us had actually been stationed at RAF Medmenham. It was, however, the parent unit for a host of small radar stations dotted around the coast, and protocol dictated that it was from

Medmenham that we were to be demobbed. We spent two full days going through the various procedures before being released into the outside world early the following morning, thereby allowing us plenty of time to reach various locations throughout the country.

Sheff and Harry were going home. Sheff to Ampton Street, WC1, just off the Gray's Inn Road, very close to Kings Cross Station, while Harry was heading for Lincoln. In my case it was not quite so simple as I didn't have a home to go to. Instead of heading for my pre-service home at Welwyn Garden City, I was in fact returning to Sussex, where I had spent the last fifteen months of my service. To realise why and to understand certain parts of my story, it will be necessary for me to describe in some detail my childhood and teenage years even though much of it is depressing and painful to recall. I had had enough varied experiences in the eighteen years prior to National Service to last a lifetime. Maybe I feel the need to get rid of some ghosts. So much has remained unsaid for so long.

Initially I set out to document the complete two years of my National Service. I wanted it to be a readable human story, rather than a mere collection of facts and figures. I knew fairly soon after leaving the RAF that I would make an early attempt at writing the story, but that first effort was abandoned very soon after it was started. Nevertheless, in preparation for another attempt at some future undefined date I compiled a list of over 100 names of people that I had encountered over the two years, complete with a brief profile of each.

This was to prove invaluable when, nine years later in 1967, a second laborious handwritten effort struggled through the first nine months of my service time before grinding to a halt. In October 2003 at the age of 66, having retired for a second time, I picked up where I had left things in 1967 and finally made it to the end. Like many of my age group I have been dragged kicking and screaming into the computer age, acquiring a keyboard speed, that, by the end of the book, just about matched my handwriting speed. The correcting and rearranging facility of word processing, however, has made the overall production considerably easier than it was in 1967. What has not been quite so easy has been the dredging up of the second part of the story from memories that go back nearly half a century

In thirty-six years my style of writing has changed, so it became necessary to re-write and improve much of the earlier text. In doing so I was totally unprepared for the amount of personal detail relating to the first eighteen years of my life that I would find it necessary to include and for the depth of feeling generated by doing so. The situation that existed during the years prior to call-up spilled over into the service period, influencing many of the happenings during the first year. Since this situation also had a major bearing on my future plans, it does not seem possible to record this very important two-year period of my life without describing the events that preceded it.

Introduction

My friends and I, back in 1955, knew that provided nothing unusual was discovered at the medical examination, we would have to serve two years of compulsory National Service in one of the three armed forces. Some of our mates or family members were either already doing so, or had completed their spell. Their stories were so varied that it was difficult to know what to believe, but in most cases they were certainly doctored to such a degree as to scare the hell out of those that were still facing National Service.

In the years soon after the war, National Servicemen had been involved in conflicts in various parts of the world, with, sadly, many not returning. In 1955, when most of my group of friends were awaiting call-up, we were not too well versed in international happenings and generally waited for the call without too many fears. If there were fears, they were directed more towards what horrors might be experienced at square-bashing rather than towards what could be in store on the larger stage. Some, not wanting any disruption to a cosy home life, were quite relieved to fail the medical. Most, if given the choice, would probably not have gone.

I had no worries about National Service. Life in general was not treating me too well, so I couldn't see anything about two years in the forces that would cause me any more problems than those that I already had.

The first ten years of my life were spent in a village in Sussex called Warnham, close to Horsham and very near to the Surrey border. My mother died from tuberculosis shortly before my eighth birthday, almost at the end of the war, after a long period of poor health. My father was in the Air Force for most of the war, and during this period I had two lengthy spells of living with relations while my mother was in hospital. After his demob from the Air Force, my father re-married and started a new life at Welwyn Garden City in Hertfordshire.

At the time of my mother's death I was living with relations in the nearby village of Broadbridge Heath. But it was not possible for this arrangement to continue on a long-term basis. As my father was still in the Air Force, I was to spend the next two years in two foster homes back in Warnham.

Following a spell of near normality in the first foster home, my already complicated early life entered a most unusual phase in the second one. The family were members of a religious sect called The Society of Dependants, founded in 1850 by John Sirgood, which nearly 100 years later was only just starting to decline. Most of the sect's operation was contained within the north-western corner of Sussex and a small area of neighbouring Surrey, although they also had chapels in Chichester, Bognor and Hove. It had a very strong following in Warnham as well as in the nearby villages of Loxwood and Northchapel.

The sect combined their religious beliefs with considerable forward-thinking business talent, owning farms, shops, bakeries and even the local garage in Warnham, with similar holdings in other villages. The various enterprises provided work for the members, and at one point the sect employed thirty-two people in Warnham alone. The shops were staffed entirely by single ladies who lived together in property owned by the sect. They were never referred to in the village by their Christian names. The only name that I can remember, Miss Madgwick, gives the whole thing a distinct Dickensian flavour. They held strong moral principals but were kindly and caring. Almost the whole day on Sundays was spent in chapel, the women wearing Quaker-style bonnets and dark clothing.

My guardians were strict but not unkind. For a healthy nine-year-old a whole day in chapel would not be an obvious first choice, particularly as the chapel was just outside of the village and we did not go home between services. Even an hourly Mint Imperial did little to ease the situation. The chapel is still there, but it is now a private house.

At its height the sect probably had around 2000 members, but its popularity gradually declined with the last chapel, at Loxwood, closing in 1984. It is likely that in around forty years or so there will be nobody left alive to remember this unique part of Sussex history.

Having been involved with The Society of Dependants, I find the subject interesting and having done some recent research to supplement my own memories I could write at greater length. This, however, is not really the right place for doing so. There is considerable information available on the Internet under the heading Cokelers, the name by which the sect was usually known. There is also a large and informative book, *John Sirgood's Way* by Peter Jerome.

It was from this unusual rural setting that, in February of the severe winter of 1947, I was transported to live with my father, stepmother and three new stepbrothers in the bustling new town of Welwyn Garden City. It was an arrangement that was full of difficulties and problems right up to the time of my entry into the Air Force early in 1956. I was two months short of my tenth birthday. This was to be my sixth home, with six different sets of people, some related, some not.

For the first two or three years the situation seemed reasonable. Despite the presence of my father, it seemed for much of the time to be a continuation of the two years in foster homes. But for the next nine years I felt totally outside of the family unit. My stepmother was a very dominant character, and as our relationship gradually deteriorated, the degree of unfairness and injustice increased in proportion. Once I had left school at the age of fifteen, I became very self-sufficient and spent as much time away from the house as possible. Some of this time was spent in the homes of friends, but the presence of a very large boys' club in the town, which opened every weekday evening plus some weekends, was my lifesaver in this difficult period. I stayed at the club until closing time, only returning home in the evening after everyone else had gone to bed.

In later years I have often given thought to my father's inability or reluctance to intervene on my behalf. At no time did we enter into any discussions concerning my position within the family. I have tended to make excuses on his behalf, bearing in mind that he had entered an established household with a family, that he had played no part in creating.

Strangely enough I embarked upon my two years of National Service expecting to return to this unsatisfactory way of life when it was all over. Five weeks into my service, however, I returned home for the standard 48-hour pass at the halfway point of basic training to find that I no longer had a bed. The message seemed fairly clear, and as further events were to unfold over the next two years, my earlier thoughts underwent several revisions during my period of service.

Acknowledgements

Shortly after Christmas 2003, armed with my recently acquired computer skills and my new e-mail address, I decided to renew a long lost contact with a friend and club-mate John Cobley. John had been in Canada for many years. Apart from a few brief snippets of information passed on from other friends, we had not been in contact for over 30 years.

It was a smart move. Following a long spell in journalism, John now teaches writing at college level for a living. On hearing of my book project he immediately volunteered his services as a proof-reader. It is thanks to a huge effort by him in totally overhauling my concept of correct punctuation, in addition to much other valued advice, that this book has made it through to this stage.

Thanks are also due to Jonathon Hook, who, in the brief period that I worked for him after my official retirement, taught me more of my basic computer skills than he probably realized. My daughter Jennifer dragged me through to the next level, taking over herself when the ageing grey matter couldn't cope with the more technical bits.

Finally, my wife Joyce, who has read everything that I have written at least twice, enduring many lengthy discussions in the process. She told me long before John did that my sentences were far too long. I should have listened.

Bibliography

Alan Titchmarsh, 1993, *The English River,* Jarrold.

Marion May, 2002, *The Story of the Dependants,* Shamley Green History Society.

John Tobler & Pete Frame, 1980, *25 Years of Rock,* Hamlyn.

Roy Humphreys, 1993, *Dover at War 1939-1945,* Alan Sutton.

The Cambridge Encyclopedia, 1994, BCA & Cambridge University Press.

Athletics Weekly, Various issues 1956-1957.

Truleigh Hill 1957. Back: 'Doc' Kinsey, Pete Mawer, John 'Geordie' Patterson and ' Sheff' (John Shefford). Author in front, on dustbin.

1.   Cardington

Somewhere, amongst the mountain of paper that inhabits every drawer and cupboard in my house and has escaped being shredded or re-cycled on the grounds of being of historic or nostalgic importance is a small brown card summoning me to a medical examination in St Albans, around the middle part of 1955.

The purpose of this examination was to determine whether I was in a fit enough state to wear the blue uniform of Her Majesty's Royal Air Force for two years' National Service, which all able bodied young men were required to do in this period soon after the end of World War Two. There were actually three choices, the Army and the Navy being the other two. The Navy was a fairly closed shop, and in the main were only taking men with a family history in the Navy. The Air Force seemed to me to be the better option of the other two.

There was always the possibility that the medical would reveal some unknown deficiency, such as flat feet or colour blindness, and some of my acquaintances seemed relieved to escape on these grounds, but unless there was a minimum height requirement that rejected my vertically challenged five feet two and a half inches, I looked fairly certain to pass. In any event, life in general was not treating me too well, so National Service was not holding any fears for me.

I would have been about three months short of my nineteenth birthday at the time of call-up. I could have applied for a deferment until after I had completed my tool-making apprenticeship at the age of twenty-one, and my employers did in fact go down this road initially. Very shortly after, however, they changed their minds and suspended my apprenticeship, making it necessary for me to register for service. I can't really blame them as I didn't want to be there and was not treating the job very seriously. I had spent my last two years of school getting a technical education and wanted to be an apprentice Draughtsman at the nearby De-Havilland Aircraft Company, along with a couple of my school mates. Nobody asked my opinion, and the tool-making job was found for me before I left school. Oddly enough I was quite good at it, and the skills that I learned during the three years of the apprenticeship that I did complete, served me well in several jobs in later life.

So off to St. Albans I went to present myself for examination. The medical passed successfully, and after a few basic intelligence tests I was asked if I had a criminal record. I had to confess to being fined seven shillings and sixpence with one and six costs for riding two on a bicycle the previous year, which caused a certain amount of mirth among the examining officers, but this wasn't on the list of major crimes in the Air Force admission handbook. All I had to do now was wait for the call.

I was now in some state of confusion concerning employment up to the time when I would be required for service, which turned out to be about four months. My employers had indicated that my apprenticeship could be resumed after National Service, if I returned as a more responsible adult, but they made it clear that they required me to find other employment until I was called up.

I managed to find a temporary packing job in a company that had two comb factories locally. This period is fairly insignificant, and other than setting the background for the period immediately prior to my call-up, the only reason that it comes into the story is that it gives me a chance to talk about Harry Hibbs, the company's most famous employee.

To anyone under the age of seventy, the name of Harry Hibbs will mean nothing, unless they are familiar with the pre-war history of Birmingham City Football Club. Harry was the van driver who operated between the two factories, but in truth he was much more than that. Between 1929 and 1936 he played in goal for England twenty-five times, while playing for Birmingham from 1924 to 1940. In 1953 he applied for permission to play in amateur football.

At the time of this story he was playing centre forward for local teams around Welwyn Garden City at the age of 50. He lived modestly in a rented house and drove a van for a living. He was no less a superstar than today's high profile, overpaid players, who seem generally unappreciative of the privileged position that they occupy. What would be the likelihood today of working in a factory alongside such a major name in football history? It certainly seems unlikely that David Seaman, David James or others from the current age will ever drive a van for a living. Harry's son Gerry was a friend of mine, and we played together in the local boys' club team. I know that this is not really relevant, but everyone likes a bit of name-dropping, and there is more coming.

The boys club, Peartree Boys' Club, to give it its full name, was a fantastic organisation, and a lifesaver to me during my teens. It was a huge club with very large premises and a full-time manager who was officially titled The Warden. I spent every evening there from Monday to Friday and also some time at weekends. The club provided all manner of activities sporting and cultural. My involvement was diverse, to say the least. I played football in the Mid-Herts. Junior League, played table tennis in the Welwyn Garden City Senior League, and took part in boxing and running training every week. I wrote stories for the Arts Festival, played 'Puck' in A Mid-Summer Nights Dream, was 'Props Man' for the annual pantomime, and took part in a Quiz League against other local youth organisations. I was even responsible for feeding and walking the club mascot, a dog named Samson, who stayed in the club overnight and went home with the warden at weekends. The Warden throughout my years at the club was George Cooper, known to everyone as Skip, and a man to whom I owe a great deal.

At this point in my life I had actually stopped playing regular football, as I had discovered that I was a far better runner than I was a footballer. I had joined the recently formed Welwyn Athletic Club and was racing on most Saturdays; track in the summer and cross-country in the winter. My heroes at this time were Roger Bannister and Chris Chataway, and it was through the boys' club, rather than the athletics club, that I had the chance to meet both of them on separate occasions during 1955.

I had been to White City the previous year and had watched Chris Chataway break the World 5000 metres record in an epic race against Russia's Vladimir Kuts. Another boys' club locally had been able to get him to speak at their club dinner, and as I was the current Hertfordshire and Bedfordshire Boys Clubs cross country champion, I was invited to meet him.

The opportunity to meet Roger Bannister came when he took part in a televised programme to publicise the work of the National Association of Boys' Clubs. As part of the programme I was selected to run in a mile race around the streets of Hammersmith. I fancied myself as a mile runner, failing by just 3 seconds to break the 5 minute barrier the previous year, while Bannister was performing his legendary exploits a minute faster. As we lined up to start, I was one of three lucky runners that Bannister, complete with microphone, chose to have a few words with. To be spoken to by the great man was one thing, but to have it recorded on television, that was incredible. We were then filmed vanishing off into the distance and again at the finish. I came third and went back to Welwyn Garden City a minor celebrity. Televisions weren't exactly widespread in those days, but a few people had witnessed my moment of glory.

I had a group of regular friends at the boys' club, and we always met up as a group and did things together at the weekends. At eighteen nobody had a girlfriend, or at least not for any length of time. When one of us was successful he would depart from the group for a time and be back two or three weeks later. For the record the hardcore members of this group were Tom Ward, Barry Chipperfield, Tony Dean, Graham Haworth, Arthur Wood and Reg Bignell. Outside of this group I had a longstanding mate from schooldays in Gerald Watchorn (Gez), who lived in a house that backed onto ours.

Welwyn Garden City was one of the earliest new towns. Housing and places of employment were increasing at an alarming rate with families being tempted away from the overcrowded areas of North London, but entertainment facilities were not growing at the same pace.

The town centre boasted just one pub, The Cherry Tree, but it was a large purpose-built pub with various sidelines, including a very popular dance hall. We spent most Saturday evenings there, doing not very much dancing but quite a bit of drinking. At that time we were stage-three drinkers, having started with Whitbread's

Forest Brown and progressed through brown and mild to stout and mild, rejecting mild and bitter on the way.

This was Teddy-Boy time, the start of the Rock and Roll era, and dance halls throughout the country were packed on Saturday evenings. The pub was near the station, a mere twenty miles from Kings Cross, making it easy for visiting groups of 'Teds' to arrive by train from various parts of Outer London in search of variety in their Saturday evening skirmishes. Fights often took place, usually in the car park and always without our group, which kept well out of it. 'Teds' in the main were fairly civilised with their violence. GBH was usually confined to participating groups, and the random attacks and muggings carried out by today's hooligans were not part of the fifties culture. Sadly the Cherry Tree is no more. The building is still there, but it now houses a Waitrose supermarket. Nobody cares about tradition and nostalgia any more.

Sunday was cinema day. There was one cinema in Welwyn Garden City, one in Old Welwyn, a couple of miles to the North, and one in Hatfield, a couple of miles to the South. We rarely ventured as far as St Albans for the cinema, which was all of seven miles away. We did however have an adventurous period where we used to catch the train to Wood Green, and go Roller Skating at Alexandra Palace. We watched our early football at Arsenal, in the days of Matthews, Lawton, Finney, and Co., or settled for Division Two stuff at nearby Luton.

This sets the scene for the day, just before Christmas, when 'the papers' arrived. I was to report to Royal Air Force Cardington, Bedfordshire, on Monday 9th January 1956. It was all about to happen.

To get to Cardington from Welwyn Garden City was a fairly simple matter. The town was on the edge of the A1, The Great North Road, and a private bus company called Birch ran a double-decker bus from somewhere on the outskirts of London to Rushden in Northamptonshire, passing the gates of Cardington Camp on the way. The distance was no more than thirty miles, so I didn't have to rush. As it happened I left home early, totally without ceremony, as though I was going off to work.

One of my three stepbrothers, Ian, who is about three years older than me, was going to work and walked part of the way down the road with me. He made an attempt to talk about my situation within the family and gave some indication that he was not happy with it. My stepmother ruled the roost; her decisions or motives were never questioned. It was the first time that anyone in the family had spoken to me along these lines and a further 48 years were to elapse before Ian and I resumed that particular conversation. In fairness, bridges were eventually repaired, or at least patched up, and my stepmother and I remained on reasonable terms, even after my father's death from a heart attack at the early age of fifty-two.

George Cooper, the boys' club leader, lived in a road called Lemsford Lane, which was close to where I would be getting the bus to Cardington, and as he was not on duty on the Monday morning, I called in to see him on the way. The club had been a very necessary second home to me, and he probably had no idea how much of an influence he and the club had had on my development as a teenager. At the club I was on the boys' council, and with my involvement in various activities was considered to be quite an important member. This involvement was providing compensation for the things that were not satisfactory in other areas of my life. Before taking the job in Welwyn, he had been warden of clubs in Derbyshire and the Isle of Wight, and was to move to a club at Haywards Heath in Sussex the following year. The next summer, while still in the Air Force, I was running in a track meeting at Haywards Heath, and was taken completely by surprise when he appeared as one of the timekeepers.

From George Cooper's house in Lemsford Lane it was a short walk to the bus stop on The Great North Road. With time to kill, I ordered a huge fry-up in the nearby transport café making a bigger dent in my cash reserves than I anticipated. I had been warned to get some cash together before embarking on my service career and had carefully accumulated the huge sum of six pounds, just over a week's wages.

The Birch bus eventually rumbled into sight and I settled down with my *Athletics Weekly* to try to ease the nerves that were beginning to take hold.

The road systems in Hertfordshire have undergone some serious changes since my epic first experience of a Birch bus journey. In 1956 we were travelling on the original A1 which has since had two updates, the latest being the current excellent A1(M). To see the old road now, no more than a country lane in front of The Waggoner's pub, it is difficult to imagine it as the lethal highway that we were warned as kids to take extra care when crossing.

The bus route to Cardington, a few miles South of Bedford, probably went through Stevenage and Hitchin, before arriving at the camp, the gates of which were very prominent and right on the main road. Engrossed in my magazine, I missed the stop completely and had to walk back from the next one.

I walked in through the gates and presented myself at the guardroom, where a very polite policeman directed me to the Reception Centre and assured me that I would be made very welcome. This I doubted, but followed his instructions to the centre, where I stared in amazement at a huge sign which said 'WELCOME TO THE RAF.' Feeling very nervous all on my own, I was just summoning up the courage to go in when an Air Force coach roared up beside me, emptied out a pile of bodies clutching holdalls and suitcases, and charged off back to Bedford Station for another lot. This was better. There were now twenty of us, and we went in en bloc.

Cardington received all new entrants, Monday to Friday, and dealt with all of the administration and kitting out, prior to despatching its newly uniformed recruits to one of five 'square-bashing' camps exactly one week later. The day on which you arrived at Cardington determined which 'square-bashing' camp you would spend the next eight weeks at.

The polite policeman at the guardroom was probably the last normal human being we would encounter during our week amongst the permanent inhabitants at Cardington. It is difficult to imagine what went on in the heads of the staff that were involved in the kitting-out and administration during this first week. Most seemed to suffer from some sort of power complex, taking full advantage of our nervousness and general lack of security. Although some very hard cases were coming into the Air Force, nobody was really sure how much power these creatures had, and how far you could go in response to their attitude. Although they were generally of fairly low rank, they were safe in their assumption that recruits in the first week of service were unlikely to respond either verbally or physically. I have read other National Service memoirs, and I know that I am not alone in my feelings on this subject.

The attitude problem started at the Reception Centre, where a humble clerk even managed to inject an unnecessary amount of aggression into the simple task of billet allocation. Worse was to follow. The twenty of us that were assigned together to a billet had the misfortune to meet an obnoxious character from whom there was to be no escape during the next week. Each billet was under the control of a very low-grade member of the permanent staff, whose function was to be a sort of imitation drill instructor and march us from point to point to collect our various items of equipment through the week. These were known as 'marshallers'. Our particular marshaller had only made one advancement in rank (to Aircrafsman1) in nearly four years of service. He insisted on being called 'staff' on all occasions and kept up a thoroughly bullying attitude throughout the week.

On reflection he was probably the right selection for the job, since we were going to have to get used to similar treatment in the weeks to come. Even though we all accepted that the real drill instructors at square bashing had to adopt this sort of attitude in order to do their jobs properly, we questioned the reason for it here. It was easier to accept the insults and bullying attitude from someone with a couple of stripes on his arm, but we found it hard to take from this miserable apology for a human being.

I have written this section three times. The first time, I actually named the individual in question, and was really insulting in my comments. The second and third versions have omitted his name and have been progressively toned down in content. The original version would probably have added more interest to the story.

This episode almost had a happy ending, as we watched in eager anticipation when a big lad from Yorkshire came very close to sorting him out. Although we were disappointed when the big fellow backed off at the last minute, it was a wise decision. A spell in the guard- room is not the best way to complete your first week in the Air Force.

Each day at Cardington resulted in a trek around different departments collecting various items of equipment and documents. As I was on the short side, to put it mildly, it had occurred to me that I could be in some difficulty on the uniform fitting scene, but since I had passed the medical, I had to assume that they were prepared for people of my height or lack of. I needn't have worried. The uniforms were all on long racks in a big hanger type building, largest on the left, shortest on the right, and we had to line up in front of our respective sizes. The bulk of the men were in a large central block with a few very big guys out at intervals to the left, and a gap of a few sizes to me on the right. Then came a surprise, not only were there uniforms shorter than mine, there was even a body shorter than mine.

We had to dress up in both uniforms, best blue and working blue, and stand on a raised area while a tailor made a chalk mark where legs or arms needed to be shortened. Two days later we returned to collect perfectly fitting uniforms. Boots, shoes, shirts, etc. all fitted without problem, the beret was OK, but the peaked cap gave some cause for concern. The cap was the last item to be issued, and by the time we reached this point, both arms were supporting a huge pile of clothing, so that all you could do was to lean forward with your head pointed in the general direction of a very unenthusiastic cap-issuer. He then made a snap size judgement and plonked a cap on your head. There were no hands free to check if it fitted OK, and we were under pressure to keep moving, so the first opportunity to find out if you had a decent fit was back in the billet, when you were able to put down the rest of your gear. By then it was too late to do anything about it. Nobody fancied talking to the horrible marshaller about it, so if the cap didn't fit, we just accepted what we had.

Haircut time arrived, and we marched in lines to the barber shop and waited our turn. Twenty hairstyles of varying kinds went in, and twenty 'short back and sides' came out. Remember, as mentioned earlier, these were 'Teddy-boy' times, and some very impressive creations ended up on the barbershop floor. I think the barbers were civilian employees, which would explain why most of the conversation was connected with football, and for very good reason. The beginning of January is traditionally the time for the third round of the FA. Cup, and the local club, Bedford Town, from the Southern League, were very big news that particular week, having done well to reach this stage. They had come out of the hat with a dream tie against Arsenal at Highbury, and the previous Saturday they had come away from London with an amazing two-all draw. The replay, at Bedford, was due on the Thursday of my Cardington week, hence the excitement in the barbers shop. Bedford Town again performed with distinction, losing by just two goals to one.

Nothing much was required of us in the evenings at Cardington, so generally we wandered off in twos and threes to the NAAFI and suffered the luke-warm beer together. It is strange how, with the vast numbers involved, it was possible to come across the same people at different stages of the two years' service. My usual partner on these trips to the NAAFI at Cardington, Derek Henry from Catford, was to reappear a few months later at St. Margaret's Bay, near Dover, where we became good mates and shifted large quantities of considerably better beer in many establishments in the Dover and Deal area. I was also aware that Sheff, whom I mentioned in the introduction, was in the next billet at both Cardington and West Kirby, before we met up at three different stations later on.

All of our preparations were completed by Friday, and just as I was viewing the prospect of spending the weekend at Cardington, I received the surprise information that I had been given a 48-hour pass. Just me. No one else in the billet had been granted this privilege. Nobody usually got home for five weeks after entering. It was explained to me by a very understanding officer that Bill Mobsby, the Secretary of Welwyn Athletic Club, had written to request my release to run in the Hertfordshire Junior Cross Country Championships.

On the Saturday before going to Cardington I had Placed 12th in the county senior championship, and had been selected as a reserve for the Hertfordshire team for the Inter Counties Championship. Bill had laid it on a bit, and said that I had a chance of winning the junior race. It was hardly the Olympics, but the RAF. were very co-operative, and it looked a good omen for the future.

It was fairly wishful thinking on Bill Mobsby's part though. On form I might have managed 4th or 5th, but due to the stresses of the past week and no training, I ended up 10th. The final twist came the following week, when Hertfordshire tried to call me up for the Inter County race. I had moved on to my square-bashing camp at West Kirby and had not passed on my new address in time for them to contact me. At 18, I would have been one of the youngest to gain senior county honours, but it is unlikely that I would have done myself justice.

2.   West Kirby

The following Monday we were due for onward transit to our square-bashing camp. My early notes state that 1500 recruits entered the RAF each week, 300 per day, and correspondingly 1500 were demobbed each week. The day of entry determined which of the five training camps you would spend the next eight weeks at. There were several options: West Kirby, on the Wirral in Cheshire and just across the Mersey from Liverpool; Padgate and Wilmslow in the Manchester area; Hednesford in Staffordshire; and Bridgnorth, on the River Severn in Shropshire.

We were bound for West Kirby, and a grim insight into the future came with the arrival of Corporal Ward, who had come down from West Kirby to escort us. He was truly frightening, at well over six feet. Everything about him was pressed, polished, blancoed and scrubbed to perfection. He positively radiated authority. Cardington was a mere practice; we were about to enter the real world, and it scared the hell out of us.

Cardington had its own station, and we lined up on the platform in strict alphabetical order, with gleaming white brand new kit bags with blue bands and our names stencilled in black. I remember seeing a kitbag go by with the name Balls stencilled on the side, and thinking that the owner would be in for a hard time later on.

We sat on the train, eight to a compartment in strict alphabetical order, came off at West Kirby Station onto trucks in strict alphabetical order, and leapt off the trucks onto the parade ground at a gallop again in the same order. The trucks drove straight on to the enormous parade ground, and we poured out of the back and literally ran, carrying kit bags, across the parade ground to form up in our alphabetical places. All this was to the accompaniment of a continual torrent of noise coming from a formidable drill instructor, whom we later came to know and fear as Corporal 'Geordie' Newton. Any hopes that Ward was a one-off were quickly dashed. Newton was equally frightening, and he was going to be involved in much of what we were heading for in the next eight weeks.

There was some reasoning in this alphabetical arrangement, as a few minutes later I became a member, along with 21 others with surnames between S and W, of hut 185, Flight 3, Smuts Squadron. At least that was the general intention. Somehow or other, however, the great system had slipped up, and in our billet of 22 bodies were two Cs and an F amongst 19 S to Ws.

After drawing our bedding, we had a few moments to take stock and make contact with our new companions. The hut was long and rectangular with eleven beds on each side, and with a tall cupboard and a small cupboard between each bed.

On my left was a grand bloke called Fred Thomas from Woolwich, and on the other side of him was the equally agreeable, fairly beefy, Mick Talbot from Tilbury. In situations such as the one we were in, groups of like-minded people generally tend to drift together, and I felt an immediate liking for these two. Fairly soon we were joined by Alan Tapson, from Aylesham in Kent, and a couple of Brummies, George Cotton and Stan Todd. George had just got married and was not too pleased at the enforced separation. He had also been a runner at some time with the Birmingham club Small Heath Harriers, so I talked him into getting going again, and he took part in a couple of the cross-country events that came up on a regular basis.

The rest of the billet was comprised of all manner of different types. Immediately to my right was a large but quiet guy called Wade, who came from Shrewsbury. He kept mostly to himself, but we came together a couple of weeks later as an unlikely team on guard duty. He wasn't the largest, however, as this honour went to Tom Tillings from Tonbridge, who had been appointed as the billet senior man, probably on the strength of his height of six feet four or thereabouts.

Next to him was Ray Smith from Isleworth, who had just completed accountancy exams, and the bottle of whisky in his locker stamped him as being a bit better off than the rest of us. With his mate Seward, who played hockey for the camp team, and a guy called Turner from Exeter, they seemed to be the aristocrats of the party.

There were two other Smiths, Anthony from Portsmouth and Sidney from Sheffield, who was one of four Yorkshiremen among the 22. One was a 17-year-old, one of two in the hut, whose surname was Worrall, but my records and memory let me down, as I can't recall his Christian name or where in Yorkshire he came from. Much the same can be said about Derek, except that his surname has gone missing. I have remembered it right with regard to the final one, however, Duncan Waddington, who was quiet, likeable and from Halifax.

Among the others were Don Cannings, from a village near Maidstone, and Graham Fowler, another from Shrewsbury. Graham had come into National Service very late, and at 26 and rapidly balding, was by far the oldest among us. Next to him was the youngest, another 17-year-old called Wagstaffe, from Northampton. Wagstaffe was just an ordinary guy with no outstanding features, until the last week at square-bashing when he managed to get himself talked into the squadron boxing team. Most of us expected him to get hammered, but he performed admirably and won his fight, and his stock rose considerably in the billet for the next few days.

This leaves three to go. On the other side of Fred Thomas was Brian Warner from Kings Lynn, and the final two were Les Willmore from Ilford and Brian Wright from Harrow. We were to share many lows and occasional highs during the next eight weeks, and in the main we all got along reasonably well together, considering the different backgrounds.

Some received food parcels from home, and the general rule relating to the sharing of additional food was usually observed, although it was possible to wake up in the middle of the night and hear the sound of paper rustling and food being craftily consumed. It was also possible on these occasions to hear a few tears being shed. Those who had perhaps had it very easy at home, found it all rather different from what they were accustomed to.

After sampling our first West Kirby meal and returning to the billet, Newton arrived, and with a few quick barks had us lined up outside the hut, from where he marched us to the NAAFI. 'You will buy three coat hangers, two padlocks, one tin of shoe polish, one tin of Brasso, one tin of blanco and two dusters', he instructed and my original six quid took another battering. One of my shoe brushes is still in use nearly 50 years later, as is one of the coat hangers on which the inscription 2782765 Taylor R.F. is just about visible.

We were given some vague advice on what was expected of us in preparing our uniform for inspection, which could happen at any time, in addition to the routine hut and kit inspection every morning. Tuesday evening was designated 'bull-night' in readiness for the really big inspection on Wednesday morning. The washing, ironing, brass polishing, and blancoing of webbing were fairly straightforward, but items such as berets and boots needed special treatment. To use today's language, the final appearance of your beret was a major factor in determining whether you looked reasonably 'cool', or whether you looked an absolute 'nerd'. To achieve the former, it was necessary first to soak the beret several times, alternately hot and cold, second to mould it into the required shape on your head while it was still wet, and third take it off carefully and leave it to dry in shape overnight. On a cold January night this was unlikely, so it meant wearing a damp beret for most of the next day.

The boots took a bit longer. The standard method was to take the lid from your tin of polish and spit into it several times. With a duster you then smeared a thick coating of boot polish over the toe caps, then with one finger in the duster you dipped it into the spit and pressing very hard, worked in the polish in a succession of tiny circles.

The idea was to completely flatten out the original dimpled surface of the toecap to produce a shiny flat surface. This took many applications to achieve. A supposed short cut was to heat up the metal handle of the stove lid until it was red hot, and with a generous layer of polish flatten out the surface with the hot metal. Nobody in our group tried it. The repercussions from ruining a pair of boots were unthinkable.

The cleaning duties in the billet were shared out fairly on a roster basis, with the main emphasis being placed upon the polishing of the lino flooring. Every person did his own bit between the beds, but the main central section, probably about 100 feet by 6 feet, had to be done as part of the roster with an item of equipment called a bumper. This consisted of a huge lump of iron on a felt pad with a moveable handle about five feet long. I hadn't seen one before, and I certainly haven't seen one since.

I devised a method where I pushed it out in front of me, and then pulled it back sharply through my legs, thereby polishing five feet in front and five feet behind in one go. There were two disadvantages. Since my vital parts were a lot closer to the floor than most peoples, I had to be careful not to do myself a mischief. Also, I couldn't see who was behind me. On one occasion Stan Todd, returning from the NAAFI with a cake in each hand, caught the bumper in full swing. Stan went one way and the cakes went the other. We abandoned the practice after this.

The days quickly fell into a routine of drill sessions, with or without rifles, at least once a day, and GCT (Ground Combat Training) most days. All of the drill sessions were with Newton, as well as some of the other activities. The effect that he had on our lives was enormous. It is very difficult to explain how one corporal can strike fear into the hearts of a flight of over 100 men. Several came into the forces as tough men in their own areas at home, but they couldn't beat the system. Any physical retaliation would result in time in the guardroom, which would result in time being added to the eight weeks at West Kirby. This of course, nobody wanted. Newton and the other Drill Instructors had the power to condemn you to an evening on fatigues in the cookhouse, whereby you lost time in keeping your equipment up to scratch. This could be for any verbal response or even for getting it wrong on the drill sessions. The fear that you could be kept beyond the eight weeks was always there.

Newton could make you look an idiot in front of the rest of the flight. He could be insulting, and he could be downright frightening. It is difficult to describe on paper. Some of the stock, and supposedly motivational, sayings used by Newton and the other corporals were either disgustingly obscene, generally offensive, or quite amusing, depending on your upbringing.

I have read reports that some recruits were upset at the amount of foul language used, not only by the NCOs, but by their billet room mates also. I do not swear much nowadays, at least only mildly and occasionally, but I certainly did in my teens, so none of this worried me, unless I was the direct recipient. I can well imagine the distress suffered by someone of a sheltered upbringing to be singled out by a drill instructor for a crude verbal blasting.

Newton was, for a variety of reasons, the most memorable figure of my entire two years' service. He had the power to strike a level of previously unknown terror into the hearts of recruits, who probably considered that they were hard men in their own right at home. His turnout was never less than immaculate; even his face shone! If you were off duty and you saw Newton approaching in the distance, you would take an alternative route in case he found something to find fault with on your uniform. Even on a Sunday, with everyone flaked out on their beds, his very entry into the room had everyone off their beds and standing to attention. When I made my first attempt to write these memoirs over thirty years ago, I said that we all hated him. In hindsight I am not sure that this is correct. We appreciated that he had a difficult job to do and that he did it well. At the end of our time at West Kirby, something was to happen that changed our perspective of him completely and made it difficult to adopt a balanced view when looking back.

The Ground Combat Training was another major part of our training, and again it was carried out by some very threatening instructors, all corporals in the RAF Regiment, the tough arm of the Air Force.

On our first session we were seated around the edges of a small room, probably about forty of us, ten to each side, waiting for the instructor to come in. In due course he arrived, making a big noisy entry and bellowing to us to be quiet in a real grade-one East End accent. As I had been living only twenty miles from London, my own accent was not too far removed from the London speech, and I usually was quite proud to pass myself off as a Londoner. Mick Talbot was sitting next to me, and as he was from Tilbury, he had much the same attitude. I leaned over to Mick and said 'How's that for a fair old London accent?' The corporal, whose name was Webb, shot across and demanded to know what I had said, assuming it to be something derogatory. When I repeated it, he took it as a criticism of his accent, of which he was very proud.

There then followed a very nasty moment when he threatened to do me very serious damage and said that I was very lucky that only his stripes prevented him from doing so. I didn't argue with that. I would have liked the chance to explain, but it was never likely to be possible. He asked where I came from, so I said 'Wellin', hoping he would think it was Welling, which is nearer to the East End than Welwyn. I certainly wasn't going to say Welwyn Garden City, which would have sounded very poofy in the circumstances. It was an awful moment, and one which comes back occasionally to haunt me.

Most of the Combat Training centred around the stripping and cleaning of our rifles, and the stripping and re-assembly of the Bren-Gun. We got to fire both for real a bit later on, and that is a story in itself.

During the first week at West Kirby our intake of 300 was assembled for a lecture by one of the senior officers, the purpose of which was questionable. We were kindly informed by the officer that there was a disreputable dance hall in the nearby town of Moreton, called The Haig, and strongly advised not to go near it. We were also advised not to have anything to do with a particular type of young lady, several of which we were informed could be seen hanging around the main gate at certain times, particularly on pay-days.

This lecture served to ensure that the dance hall continued to receive a large slice of its annual turnover courtesy of Royal Air Force West Kirby, and it also produced a large number of casual strollers in the vicinity of the main gate. With recruits confined to camp for the first two weeks, it has been said that business was sometimes carried out through the chain link fencing.

Also at this gathering, all sportsmen of county standard were asked to come forward and add their names to a register as possible members of station sports teams. I got my name down on the cross-country list, and in due course was summoned to meet a Flight Lieutenant Speller, who was in charge of the camp team. I was instructed to report to the gym at 2pm each afternoon for training, which suited me down to the ground. On the first afternoon I reported to the PTI (Physical Training Instructor) who was captain of the team. He was a Scot called Peter McKaill, who was a member of the permanent staff and also belonged to the local Wirral Athletic Club.

We had quite a useful team, but it was not as strong as I expected, considering the number of young people between 18 and 22 coming into the Air Force each week. Also because of the weekly movements, the team was changing all of the time. Initially the team star was Dave Coward of Southgate Harriers, but he was more than adequately replaced later by Bob Hemmings (Peterborough A.C.), the Northants senior cross-country champion. Another decent runner to arrive later was Tom O'Reilly, from Springburn Harriers in Scotland, who held the Scottish steeplechase record a couple of years later. Other team members were John Blackaby (Ilford A.C.), Pat McGinn (Eton Manor A.C.), Barry Wooding (Farnham A.C.), Peter White (Liverpool Pembroke A.C.), and Peter Kirkton (Northampton H.). Corporal McKaill supervised the training sessions, which were generally group runs around the Wirral countryside. The area around Thurstaston Common was a large National Trust area of gorse and open moorland and was very inspiring, even on a cold January afternoon.

After the first two weeks, when we were allowed off the camp individually, I got in several runs of close to ten miles at the weekends and was getting pretty fit. On other occasions we did circuit training in the gym, and occasionally I joined in with the boxers, having had experience of this type of training at the boys club.

During the first two weeks, the only way to get off the camp was to go to church in West Kirby. Several of us went on both Sundays, and a coach was laid on for this purpose. Regrettably I have to say that escape, rather than worship, was our main motivation. As it happened the trips were very pleasant. The Methodist Church was an impressive building with a balcony, and we were warmly welcomed by the local members of the congregation. After the service we were invited to spend an hour or so with the youth fellowship, and to make us feel at home, we were asked to stand up individually and give our Christian names, our home town, and any notable facts about it. Welwyn Garden City isn't noted for much, but it was, and still is, known throughout the country as the home of Shredded Wheat, and that really was all I could think of.

Once we were allowed out with no strings attached, we started with a peaceful trip into West Kirby for a couple of drinks, but after that we didn't go into West Kirby again. I have never been back to the area since, so I have no recollection of the town at all. On the first weekend that we were able to go out, we headed straight for the 'disreputable' Haig Dance Hall at Moreton and continued to do so on successive weekends. In eight weeks we didn't catch a bus once. We went everywhere by taxi, despite a weekly pay packet of just twenty-four bob. Fleets of taxis lined up outside the main gate, and the fares were cheap. We piled five or six into each taxi, probably making it cheaper than the bus and with no waiting.

With pay at one pound twenty in modern language, if we learned anything in those early weeks it was how to make a small amount of money last as long as possible. We probably got through half of it on our big night out on Saturday, by the time we had paid for taxi fares, admission to the dance hall, and a probable minimum of four or five pints of Birkenhead Brewery's finest. More taxi fares and more booze on Sunday took a bit more, and the rest had to be carefully spread out over the remainder of the week.

The priority over the rest of the week was not alcohol but food. We were getting the basic three meals a day, but we were putting in a lot of outdoor exercise, and it was extremely cold up there on the Wirral in January. We were always hungry. During the evenings we were able to buy additional food in the NAAFI, but in the daytime, a very agreeable place to supplement the food rations was the Salvation Army Canteen. In the NAAFI the staff had a job to do, and the service was generally fairly impersonal. The Salvation Army Canteen was altogether different. Bearing in mind that most of us were experiencing something very different from our normal way of life and were in need of a bit of sympathetic understanding, the Salvation Army ladies ran an oasis of calm and kindness in the middle of a hard environment. The two months at West Kirby shaped my feelings for the Salvation Army for the rest of my life. I admire their work and general outlook, and am pleased to be a regular supporter.

If the twenty-four bob didn't last the week, it meant that we had to fall back on our reserves, this being the cash that we had come into the forces with. I had to be very careful in this respect, as I hadn't managed to accumulate a great deal. I was very mindful of the fact that at the halfway point of square bashing we were due to receive a 48-hour pass and were entitled to go home for the weekend. I had no idea if the remains of my savings would be sufficient for the train fare to Welwyn Garden City.

After about three weeks at West Kirby, I was lucky enough to get a three-day break to run for the station team in the No.22 Group Cross Country Championship at Cardington. We travelled down on the Tuesday, raced on the Wednesday, and travelled back on the Thursday.

Number 22 Group included all five square-bashing camps, plus Cardington and a few others. This meant that the best athletes from an Air Force population of around thirty or forty thousand would be taking part. Prior to our departure we paraded in our athletic kit before the Commanding Officer, who wished us well, and immediately on our return we had to get dressed up and parade before him again to be congratulated on our second place in the team competition. On my arrival back in the billet to get changed back into uniform, Newton came in and asked what had happened. When I told him he said 'You didn't get a 48 then' and actually smiled. I felt honoured.

At Cardington we were housed in billets that hadn't been used for some time, and although they had the old-fashioned black stoves the same as at West Kirby, they had not been in recent use and it was very cold indeed. It was probably the only time in my life that I have slept in pyjamas and a track-suit.

The race itself was over the extremely heavy Cardington course that had been used for the previous year's National Championship, and contained a fair amount of ploughed field, something that today's runners very rarely have to contend with. I finished 17th in a field of around seventy runners, well behind the winner, Sergeant Bill McMinnis from RAF Padgate. Bill McMinnis was a star both in and out of the forces. The previous year, at the age of forty, he had won both of the country's major marathon events with a best time of 2hrs 26mins, an excellent time now let alone fifty years ago. He was also part of the legendary Sutton Harriers team from Lancashire that won the National Cross Country team title four times between 1947 and 1951, and finished second on the other occasion. McMinnis placed in the top thirty each time, with a best position of 24th.

For our second place in the team competition we were presented with silver plated ashtrays with the No.22 Group crest in the centre. The two non-scorers in the eight-man team received medals. For some reason, which I probably understood at the time, I swapped my ashtray with a drill corporal called O'Brien, who was one of our non-scorers. I doubt if at the age of eighteen, I was as aggressively anti-smoking as I am today. I probably thought that the medal looked to be a more fitting award than the ashtray. O'Brien, who ran for the Glasgow club Maryhill Harriers, was delighted with the exchange.

Back in the routine at West Kirby, my athletic training was causing me a few problems in other areas. I was missing drill and combat training sessions, and inevitably making a few wrong moves. This led to a couple of evenings on cookhouse fatigues and consequently put me under pressure in keeping my uniform in inspection condition.

I think that probably a certain amount of additional labour was needed in the cookhouse every evening, and the onus was on the drill corporals to provide it. Whilst some of the jobs obviously needed doing, there didn't seem to be much merit in washing out giant sized greasy jam and baked-bean tins in cold water and with no form of soap or powder. I don't think re-cycling had been invented in 1956.

On my second visit, the job was more productive as I was consigned to the vegetable room. I pushed open the door of the dimly lit room, which was probably about eight feet square, and could see nothing but a huge mound of cabbage taking up about half of the floor space. A closer inspection revealed a body, dressed as I was, in green denim overalls sitting in the middle of the pile. 'What are we supposed to do?' I asked my new buddy. He explained that most of the cabbage was useless, but if you searched carefully, every now and then you came across a good bit that could be used for tomorrow's dinner. This we did for about an hour and a half, throwing all of the usable bits across the room into a tin bath placed near the door.

Just as we were knocking off after this session, a fellow internee carrying an enormous tray of bacon came past. The bacon was laid out on the tray in rows with each edge neatly overlapping the next rasher, a real work of art. This was ready to go into the oven for next morning's breakfast, but on his way through, the unfortunate bacon carrier slipped on the newly scrubbed and disinfected floor and ended up on his back among a heap of bacon.

The corporal cook was not amused, and what happened next, with the passage of nearly fifty years seems improbable. But this is how I wrote it on my last attempt in 1967, so I will have to stick with it. 'Don't just sit there', he bellowed, 'Pick it all up and lay it out again and be bloody quick about it'. This is what was done. And even after witnessing this, not one of us even remotely considered passing up on the bacon next morning.

At the halfway point in the eight weeks training the 48-hour pass arrived, giving me problems on two fronts. First, I didn't have enough of my cash reserve left to cover the train fare, and second was the problem of how welcome I would be at home. I think it was generally thought that the Air Force would keep me out of the way for a couple of years, and with a bit of luck at the end of it I would have either signed on for a longer period, or have found somewhere else to live. The absence of my bed seemed to confirm this! Whilst I didn't necessarily want to go home, I didn't want to stay virtually alone at West Kirby. There was a life that I was part of back in Welwyn Garden City that I wanted to keep contact with. I also knew that I had been entered for the Southern Junior Cross Country Championship at Windsor on the Saturday.

My very good mate Fred Thomas solved the first problem and lent me the balance of the train fare. I don't know if I ever paid him back, I hope I did. Sitting here writing this from a distance of almost half a century produces some strange emotions. Blokes come into your life for eight weeks and then vanish, never to be heard of again. Fred was a very decent guy. Perhaps he will get to read these memories and let me know if I have a long-standing debt to honour.

Anyway, I took the bull by the horns and survived a weekend at home. On the Saturday afternoon I had a very poor race at Windsor finishing 130th out of 250 runners, well down on what I was hoping for. In the evening I joined my mates for the ritual Saturday evening at the Cherry Tree and travelled back to Liverpool on Sunday evening, arriving back just as the dawn was breaking over Lime Street Station. Not a pretty sight!

Liverpool in the fifties looked grimy and run down, but I suppose this could be said about many British cities in what was basically a rebuilding period so soon after the war. To be fair, Liverpool had more than it's fair share of problems.

On the Monday that we reported back to Smuts Squadron, so did three hundred others, as the new intake arrived from Cardington that afternoon. We were no longer the newest recruits in the squadron, which did us a power of good. We took great delight in telling the newcomers how grim it all was and strictly speaking it was pretty grim. We were very small fish in what seemed to be a very large and sometimes frightening pond. For those of us who lived near to large cities, it was probably easier to adapt than it was for those who came from remote villages, and it should be remembered that life in the fifties was considerably more insular than it is today. Very few people had ordinary telephones let alone mobile phones. Families with cars were an exception rather than the norm. Some-eighteen-year olds were coming into the forces with very little experience of life outside of their own small circle of operation. If anyone was not particularly quick at picking up some of the drill or gunnery operations, the corporals would hound them unmercifully and continually ridicule them in front of the rest of the unit.

I came in for an occasional session from Newton during rifle drill. Our rifles were fairly heavy, at least for someone my size they were, with the result that I invariably found my arm straying from the regulation ninety degrees that the rifle was supposed to be held at. Consequently my rifle ended up at a different angle to everyone else's and the next thing I knew was that Newton would be marching alongside me. Initially he would say nothing, his very presence there being unnerving enough. Finally he would bend over while still marching, reducing his height by some 12 inches, to put his mouth right against my ear.

He would then say with a loud rasping voice 'Is your rifle heavy airman' to which you had to reply 'No corporal' while trying to remain calm. He would then say 'Then get the bloody thing at the right angle unless you want to spend the evening in the effing cookhouse'. It is difficult to describe this adequately in print, but anyone who has been on the receiving end will recognise the scene immediately. All of his considerable collection of stock phrases and sayings were delivered with a great degree of menace. Newton was just one of perhaps two dozen drill instructors, each with a hundred or so recruits to get into shape and some were worse than others. The effect on the recruits varied, but there was a suicide around my period at West Kirby.

One morning at breakfast as we sat examining the new intake, feeling very superior, I was astonished to see a familiar face. Among those queuing for breakfast was 'John Nick', one of my group from the boys' club at Welwyn Garden City. His real name was John Nicholson, but we abbreviated his surname to distinguish him from other Johns in the club. When I left home five weeks ago I had no idea that he was due for call up, now here we were 200 miles from home in the same cookhouse. Strangely he was the only one of our group that I maintained regular contact with after the forces. Five years later he was best man at my wedding, and my wife Joyce (who doesn't come into the story for another ten months) was matron of honour at his wedding. We kept in touch for another ten years or so, but then drifted apart after a foolish minor disagreement. I've no idea where he is now.

Life for the second part of square bashing carried on much as before, scrubbing, polishing, rifle drill, ordinary drill, combat training, physical training sessions, plus more scrubbing and polishing. One Monday the whole flight of 100 was assembled in our billet to be told the news that the blood transfusion unit was on the camp and would be receiving donations from our flight the next day. The sergeant in charge of our flight, Sergeant Rogers, was slightly less menacing than Newton, but had a very good line for ensuring maximum donations: 'There are only three reasons for which you will not give blood' he started, 'One is that you have had jaundice and this unfortunately I can do nothing about. The second is that you are under the age of eighteen. I know full well that we only have half a dozen seventeen-year-olds in this flight, and I am temporarily advancing your birthdays to tomorrow. The only other reason is that you are scared. Hands up anyone who is scared'.

The bravest man in the flight put his hand up. Sgt.Rogers was completely off-guard for a minute, as he had banked on 100 per cent attendance. 'You 'orrible little man' he stormed. 'OK, you can march them all down' he said, hoping this might provoke a change of heart. The following morning we were marched down in extremely accomplished fashion by the rebel, much to the disappointment of Sgt.Rogers, who would have laid bets upon him making a balls-up of it.

Most of us would probably not have volunteered to give blood, given the choice, but we may have done if we had realised that there wasn't very much to it at all. I laid on the bed with a tube leading underneath to a bottle which was out of sight. As people came and went on the bed next to me, I was beginning to have visions of a large container under the bed with about half of my blood in it. In the end a nurse came and told me that the blood had stopped coming at three quarters of a pint, so they were giving up and calling it a day at that. I suppose that was fair since I was probably less than three quarters of the size of most of the others. In fact, on today's regulations I probably wouldn't have been allowed to give blood under the minimum weight rules. At my medical before entering the RAF, my weight was a mere 7 stone 7 pounds stripped!

As it was Tuesday, that evening was the major 'bull night'. As cleaning operations got underway, blood-deficient blokes were dropping like flies and having to be dumped on their beds while the rest of us got on with it.

This seems to be the time for clearing up the medical agenda. The next item consisted of injections against what was never explained to us, plus a vaccination which proved to be a bit painful and resulted in a dead arm for a couple of days. The day after the injections Smuts Squadron held a cross country championship, where a guy called White, from the Liverpool club Pembroke A.C., and I ran the four miles with our left arms hanging down by our sides, coming in together for joint first place.

The injection procedure itself provided one of those semi-comic situations that National-Servicemen remember forever. We lined up outside a large hut with doors on each of the long sides and on entry removed all clothing down to waist level. There was probably about fifty of us in the hut at a time and as one went out, one went in. We gradually moved up the queue watching everyone else getting jabbed before it came to our turn. Immediately after the injections, we were shot out of the other door into the February snow, still stripped to the waist, to perform the quickest dressing operation of the whole two months. We were actually well practiced at the quick dressing routine as it happened.

Newton would have us all assembled, in 'working blue', in ranks, outside of the five billets that comprised Flight 3. He would then shout 'P.E. kit', whereupon we all dived off into our billets to re-appear extremely quickly in vests, shorts and plimsolls. No sooner had we re-formed in ranks, the next order was 'best-blue' and we were back in the billets changing into our best uniforms complete with shoes and peaked cap. Then it was back in again to re-appear in our original working uniforms, boots and berets. God help the slowest! The fear of not only being last, but last by several seconds defies description. At best it was a verbal hammering by the merciless Newton, at worst it was a cookhouse job.

The final part of the medical procedure was what was known as an FFI (Free From Infection) inspection, which required the Medical Officer to make a visual inspection of our most private and treasured possessions, to determine if any unsavoury diseases were lurking therein. We lined up at the end of our beds, in two rows facing each other, clad only in boots, socks, trousers and braces. On the command 'trousers down' from Newton, we slipped off our braces and our trousers dropped around our ankles to reveal 22 assorted sets of equipment. The sight was beyond description. We fell about laughing until a quick bark from Newton sobered us up in no time. The M.O. bent almost double and then completed a quick inspection of two rows of tackle with fortunately nobody having anything that they shouldn't have had, although the M.O. probably had a backache.

Not everything at West Kirby was bad and one of two events were arranged to lighten the gloom. One Sunday a few of us were lounging around in the billet doing nothing in particular, when Newton appeared and astonished us by asking if anyone wanted to go flying that afternoon.

He raked up about thirty of us from the five billets and we were taken by coach to Harwarden (pronounced 'Harden') just inside the Welsh border, near Chester, where we enjoyed a fifteen-minute trip in an RAF Anson, my first flight.

The officer in charge of social and general morale-building events was a very pleasant bloke called Pilot Officer Ashcroft, who was very keen on traditional jazz music, which was at a high point of popularity in the 1950s. It was therefore appropriate that the two events that he organised during our eight-week stay were a trip to a theatre in Liverpool to see the Ken Collyer band, and a visit to the camp by Laurie Gold and his Pieces of Eight with singer Gerry Brereton.

There was also the Astra Cinema on the camp. One of the films showing at the time was the Sigmund Romberg story *Deep in My Heart*. During a Cyd Charisse dance routine the audience made so much noise that the officer in charge stopped the film and refused to carry on until the noise had subsided.

Pilot Officer Ashcroft also had some responsibility for sport. His largest task every eight weeks was to assemble a Smuts Squadron boxing team for a tournament between the four squadrons, Smuts, Roosevelt, Churchill and Trenchard. It was my misfortune to be taking part in a boxing training session as an alternative to running, when he made one of his visits to the gym. Seeing me coping quite adequately with a punch ball, and skipping in true boxing fashion, his eyes lit up, as he needed someone at a very light weight to match a boxer from one of the other squadrons.

It took me a long time to talk my way out of it. I had three tournament fights between the ages of thirteen and fifteen, winning the first two but getting a pounding in the third one. At this point, I decided that I didn't want to be a boxer any more, but continued to take part in the training at the boys' club. Pilot Officer Ashcroft tried his best to persuade me and he just might have succeeded, as he had far more respect among the recruits than any of the corporals or sergeants. I figured that if one of the other squadrons had a very small boxer, there was a likelihood that he was a regular at the sport and knew what he was doing. In any event, I couldn't see him being as small as me. I could still remember the previous pounding well enough not to fancy another one.

I was getting plenty of cross-country races, with 1956 starting off with ten races in as many weeks. The next Air Force race to come up was an area championship, which served as a qualifier for the overall RAF Championship towards the end of the cross-country season. This was at Shawbury in Shropshire, just north of Shrewsbury, which was not a great distance from West Kirby. A thirty-seater RAF coach took our team of nine down and back in the day. I finished 36th in a field of around 150, which was not good enough for me to qualify for the RAF final. My memories of this event are vague, but I do have recorded that the course contained the largest and longest hill that I had so far encountered in my short running career. I know that I have only four times in over fifty years of racing had to walk uphill in a race, this being the first of those four occasions! It wasn't only me that suffered. Sergeant Bill McMinnis and Colin French, who were first and second in the Group race at Cardington, were fifth and sixth this time. French, from the North London club Shaftesbury Harriers, was a major star on the Air Force athletics scene as will be seen when the story moves into my second year.

There was also a West Kirby camp championship, where I placed second to Bob Hemmings, collecting a very nice medal in the process. The following day we had a race against a very strong Liverpool University team, on their course at Sefton Park. We took a real hammering, but probably would have still been beaten if we hadn't raced the previous day, although maybe not quite so comprehensively.

Towards the end of square bashing, as part of our training, we had to do a session of guard duty. We patrolled in pairs, two hours before midnight and two hours after. My partner was the silent man Wade, from the next bed and we had a fairly roving assignment over a designated area probably about half a mile square. The two hours before midnight were no problem. We drew eight o'clock to ten o'clock, a period when the camp was still lit up, the NAAFI and cinema were still in full swing and plenty of people were about. After an hour or so wandering around, doing routine checks on buildings that were not in use during the evening, we followed what had become an established ritual on guard duty.

The procedure was to enter one of the billets on the area and stand at one end and shout 'anyone here from Somerset' or wherever was applicable, in my case Hertfordshire, in Wade's case Shropshire. If anyone answered, it was then a question of 'whereabouts', followed by 'Do you know so and so' if the right answer was received.

At ten o'clock we went back to the guardroom to be relieved and we were permitted to sleep until our next session, which was two till four. A room had been laid out with beds for this purpose, but it seemed that we were not expected to sleep all that soundly as all of the mattresses had been removed. I am afraid that in four hours I failed to master the art of sleeping on the bare springs of an RAF bed.

At two o'clock Wade and I stepped out into the night to commence our second stint, an odd looking pairing with him a well-built six-footer and me a skinny five feet two and a half. With a whistle and a truncheon between us, we set off to defend our territory.

I have never been as cold as I was up there on the Wirral in 1956. For anyone not familiar with the geography of this part of the world, the Wirral is a rectangular lump of land roughly twelve miles wide at the top and twenty miles long. It lies between the North-Wales coast and Liverpool, and has water on three sides. To the East is the River Mersey, and to the West is the very wide estuary of the River Dee, which flows down to Chester just below the Wirral. West Kirby, for want of a better description, is on the top left hand corner and it's very exposed indeed. This particular night was one of the worst. Within fifteen minutes of our leaving the guardroom, it was snowing heavily.

The camp was in total darkness, and the artistic merits of the white snow against a black landscape were lost on us. After a few checks on the larger buildings, we headed for a large covered drill area, which was enclosed on three sides. It seemed a sensible place to be in the circumstances. The area doubled as a car park during off-duty hours, and we reckoned we could spend a fair bit of time checking car security. It wasn't much warmer there and what happened next I find hard to believe even now, bearing in mind the fear element that governed most of our movements. Wade and I were harbouring similar thoughts and within a few minutes we were laid out on adjacent beds in the comparative comfort of hut No 185. Shortly before four o'clock we crept out of the back door, doing a quick circuit of the major buildings, before reporting back to the guardroom at the end of the shift. I don't for one minute imagine that this was an original idea of ours, but to this day I am astonished that we had the nerve to do it.

Every weekday morning, after breakfast and before the first session of drill, or whatever, we lined up in ranks outside the billets for post distribution. As we were stationed miles from home, cut off from all of our normal routines and separated from families, girl friends and in some cases wives, mail from the outside world was a very important factor. I didn't receive a single letter from home during those first two months; in fact I only received two letters from that source in the whole of the two years, but I was getting regular mail from two people. One was a girl in Bristol, which will need some explaining, the other was Chris Brunning, a good friend and my coach at Welwyn Athletic Club.

In the previous two years my summer holiday had been with the boys' club at a large permanent camp-site at Orcombe Point, near Exmouth in Devon. Several clubs were there at the same time, our spell usually coinciding with that of a girls' club from Bristol. The first year, when I was seventeen, I managed to spend three days in Exmouth Hospital. I was being tossed up in the air from a blanket held by at least a dozen people, who were managing to get my seven and a half stones up to incredible heights. On one occasion, however, I came out of the blanket at an angle. While the others were scrambling to get to me, I was making a temporary exit from the world several feet away.

This was during our second week, the girls from Bristol having gone home at the weekend. While in hospital I received a letter from a girl called Marlene, who I had met the previous week and who suggested in her letter that we write to each other. We started to write about sixteen months before I went into the forces, and we continued for a total of about three years. We were both at Exmouth the following year, but somehow the romantic involvement didn't take off. Through our very regular correspondence, however, we did become very good friends, and her letters were extremely important to me at that time in my life.

Chris's letters were also important and much appreciated. Not only did he send me coaching advice, but he also used to send results of all of the club's fixtures in fantastic detail. Every club athlete's position, time, or distance, in every event. He was the club's record keeper; perhaps he was grooming me to take over! I looked forward to his letters, as I was very committed to the Welwyn Athletic Club, and tried to get to their events during my service time whenever I could.

Everyone else was getting letters on a regular basis, and the letters from Marlene and Chris at least made me feel as if I had someone out there in the big world outside of the Air Force.

We were coming towards the end of our time at West Kirby, but there were two major events still to come. On the combat training front we had learned all there is to know about cleaning and firing both rifle and Bren-gun, and stripping down and re-assembling the Bren, but we hadn't yet fired either of them for real. The time had arrived and we were duly marched down to the rifle range on two successive days to be supervised by the fattest sergeant that I've ever set eyes upon.

The rifle came first. About a dozen fired at a time with another three rows lined up behind ready to fire. The noise was tremendous, and I have to admit to being extremely nervous, expecting the 'kick' from the rifle to leave my shoulder detached from the rest of my body.

At a command from the large sergeant we took aim, and on a further command squeezed the trigger into the first pressure stage ready to fire. The silence lasted just a couple of seconds, but instead of the combined racket of twelve rifles firing together, there was the noise of a single shot as the poor guy on the end of the row let loose the first one all on his own. If he was nervous before, he was probably twice as bad after the large sergeant had finished with him.

The targets were set fairly close to each other about twenty five yards away. When we finally got to blast off our five rounds, the result was chaos. I had five shots on my target, but I am not convinced that they all came from my rifle.

Compared to the rifle, the Bren was a bit more exciting. We each had fifteen rounds, which we were supposed to fire in five short bursts of three. I got a bit carried away and by the time the shouts of the corporal beside me had got through, I had pumped about thirteen rounds into and past various targets. My own target ended up with about eight holes in it.

After our spell of action, we had to do a turn in the armoury loading up the clips with fifteen rounds ready for the next lot. That was the general idea, but as most of us had got nowhere near fifteen shots on target, we shoved a couple of extras in for good measure.

The other major exercise of note was two days of reliability and initiative tests, which despite the cold, turned out to be quite enjoyable. On the first day we were split into groups of about fifteen or so, with each group being allocated a map reference. Each of the references was for a building of some note, about ten miles from camp, with our mission being to arrive there on foot, at exactly mid-day and collect some information relative to the building, before returning to camp also on foot.

There were some rules to be observed. We had to march in single file with a leader some 25 yards ahead and another bringing up the rear a similar distance behind. On no account were we to enter any shop, pub, or building other than our final destination, and we were not to use any other mode of progression than walking. We were issued with leather waistcoat type jackets, camouflage anoraks and two sandwiches and were expected to take about six to seven hours.

We set off at 9am in a steady drizzle of wet snow. I would like to be a bit more positive than I am about which direction we were taking, but I have always imagined that we were heading down the Wirral in the general direction of Heswall. The map reference was for a hospital, which would have been on the right hand side of the road travelling south, with a sewage farm just before it on the other side of the road. However, lengthy inspection of current Ordnance Survey maps has failed to turn up such a combination, but things change over such a long period and perhaps neither the hospital or the farm are there any more.

With some fairly speedy walking we located the hospital with about three quarters of an hour to spare, having been a bit over-anxious not to arrive later than the set time. The problems now were twofold. The immediate need was for more food, the two sandwiches having been seen off at least an hour ago and not proving to be very satisfying at that. We knew that there were spotters out all over the various routes and we didn't want to get caught entering anywhere to buy food, not that there was anywhere to enter.

Someone somewhere was looking out for us, as the very next vehicle along the road was a mobile grocer's shop. This is not the sort of thing that you would expect to see on the road in the twenty-first century, but they were quite commonplace in the nineteen fifties. We flagged it down and bought what we needed without actually setting foot in it. This was after all a reliability and initiative exercise. We were probably expected to last all day on two sandwiches, so if we weren't being very reliable, at least we were showing initiative.

The burning question now was what we were going to do for over half an hour out in the countryside? The need for a decision was being made more urgent by an increase in the volume of white stuff falling from the sky. The only building in sight, apart from the hospital, was a small wooden shed a couple of hundred yards back down the road, which represented the control centre of the gentleman in charge of the sewage farm.

He was somewhat surprised, to say the least, after a knock on his door, to be confronted by a motley crew of 15 airmen asking to share his refuge, but seemed glad of the company and welcomed us in. We just about managed to squeeze in and find enough floor space to sit on, while we chatted to our new buddy for half an hour. On reflection, it probably wasn't the first time he had played host to the Air Force, since the hospital was most likely used as a reference point on a regular basis.

The smell outside as we approached the sewage farm hut was none too special, but it was nothing compared to the smell inside once the old boy lit his pipe up. With a few of ours lighting cigarettes, you could hardly see across the hut.

At five to twelve we headed off into the snow again. The plan now was for two of our group to present ourselves at the hospital reception, where, by pre-arrangement, an official would come and provide us with some facts relating to the hospital. These later had to put together in essay form as part of the exercise. Fred Thomas and I had drawn the short straws, or maybe long straws in view of the amount of snow falling outside, and presented ourselves to reception not looking quite our best in our snow-covered boots and green denim overalls. The official was very helpful and by twelve twenty we were on the road again.

A couple of miles into the return journey, we rounded a corner and were taken aback to find an identical group, sitting on benches outside a country pub, seeing off tankards of Birkenhead Brewery's finest. They had probably used the same line of initiative that we had with the mobile grocer. Surprisingly we resisted the urge to join them, and slogged it back to camp in good time for the evening meal.

The next day's exercise was a much more military style affair. The whole intake was divided into two groups, one of 100 and one of 200. The group of 100, of which I was a member, was issued with miniature sandbags and marched to the top of Thurstaston Hill, about three and a half miles away. At a given time we were to fan out and proceed back to camp by any route that we wished. At the same time, the group of 200 were released from the camp with the purpose of intercepting us and relieving us of our sandbags by any means necessary.

I had the advantage of a small amount of local knowledge, as a lot of our afternoon training runs were in this area and a very nice area it is too, even under several inches of snow as it was on that particular day. Three of us from hut 185 kept together, and we were making good progress up till we caught sight of the enemy. Right at the point where they started to close in on us stood a large country house with extensive grounds, including a lake and large areas of rhododendron bushes. Faced with possible capture the three of us dived over the wall and took cover in the bushes.

Unfortunately a few others copied us and were spotted by our opponents, resulting in several scrambles in the bushes and a few chases around the lake, before the owners called in the police and added a whole new dimension to the exercise. The area before we actually reached the house I have always known as Thurstaston Common, but reference to recent guides shows also an adjacent area called Royden Park. The only large estate that I can find in the vicinity is Frankby Hall, which is listed as the 19th century home of Sir Thomas Royden. Well, Sir Thomas, if you were looking down on that cold afternoon in February, please accept our apologies for the havoc that we were causing in what seems to be your garden.

After several narrow escapes and much crawling about in the snow, the three of us got through feeling pretty pleased with ourselves, only to find that we had been well beaten in the race to be first back by a most unlikely candidate. Brian Warner, from our hut, who occupied a bed on the other side of Fred Thomas to me, came from somewhere near Kings Lynn in Norfolk. Mainly because of his very rural Norfolk accent, he was looked upon as a bit of a country lad by us town dwellers. It transpired that he had taken the most direct route back, and on every challenge for his sandbag he claimed to have been relieved of it right at the beginning, and was just heading back to camp. Since this seemed most likely, they all believed him.

A couple of days later I was back in the same area for my final cross country race at West Kirby, which was against the local club, Wallasey Athletic Club. They had a very promising 16-year-old called Ron Barlow, who was the Cheshire Youth Champion and was to place highly in the National Championship that year. He went on to become a major star in Northern events for quite a few years.

Barlow and his club mate, Ian McIvor, went into the lead early on, with Bob Hemmings following. I made my usual cautious start and by four of the five miles had worked through into fourth place, with the others in sight. With less than a mile to go I noticed the two Wallasey runners going off course, with Bob Hemmings taking the same route. I was close enough to shout to Bob, who realised his mistake and quickly came back onto the course about thirty yards ahead of me. I started to gain on him, and as I passed he surprisingly did not respond. I got by to come in a lucky winner. Barlow and McIvor took longer to get back on course and ended up further down the field. They were not too pleased, but going off course is a fact of life in cross-country running. Twice the previous year I had gone off course when in the lead in junior races, so I wasn't over concerned about claiming victory this time. We all had a free meal in the NAAFI afterwards, which may or may not have been some consolation for the Wallasey guys.

Our training exercises were coming to an end, but a very significant event was to occur before our time at West Kirby came to a close. This was the death of Marshall of the Royal Air Force Lord Trenchard. Of the four notable figures from history who have given their names to the training squadrons, only Trenchard had a direct involvement with the Air Force. Whilst Churchill, Roosevelt and Smuts were leaders of state in times of considerable military action, it is doubtful if anyone's death, other than the Queen's perhaps, could have been of greater importance to the Royal Air Force than that of Lord Trenchard. My earlier notes for this story recorded that a four-hour parade in the snow would ensure that his memory would be preserved by the current intake at RAF West Kirby, and we made rather irreverent remarks to the effect that he might have hung on for a couple of weeks. But make no mistake, he was a very major figure in Air Force history.

He commanded the Royal Flying Corps in World War 1 and played a prominent part in the establishment of the Royal Air Force in 1918, becoming its first Air Vice Marshall during the 1920s. This was followed by a further career as Commissioner of the Metropolitan Police, where he founded the Hendon Police College. All of this was totally unknown to most of the young people paying their respects on that cold parade ground in 1956, including me. If this sounds as if it has been lifted straight from the encyclopaedia, well it more or less has, and although I am trying to describe most of the events of the time in a light-hearted manner where possible, the serious matters have to be afforded the true level of respect.

Following this, hut 185 settled down to await the final weekend with some enthusiasm, despite the prospect of the passing out parade on the Monday. We were desperate to get outside of West Kirby's gates once and for all, and to consign Newton to the far back corners of our memory. Looking back on it all from such a large time gap, there is a tendency to romanticise a bit and think perhaps that it wasn't all that bad after all. Many people have written many words about square bashing, much of it recent, as the newly retired find time suddenly available. There is a tendency to let nostalgia overtake reality, but it is possible now to appreciate the need for the harshness of the regime, something that we were unable to do at the time. When I made my previous attempt to write this story back in 1967, I didn't appear to be under any illusions about how unpleasant much of it was, so perhaps I had better trust my judgement from closer to the actual happenings.

It was therefore with a certain amount of apprehension that we received rumours that Newton was organising a celebration booze-up for the flight on Saturday evening. These were confirmed when

Newton stopped me in my tracks on the way to the NAAFI one evening. Fearing the worst, I was a bit surprised when he said 'Are you going to the flight piss-up on Saturday?' Conversation with him was always a minefield, so I kept it to the minimum by saying 'Yes corporal'. 'Good' he said, and marched off without any further explanation. But the following morning we received details, and on Saturday evening two coach loads set off for the as yet unknown delights of New Brighton.

I knew nothing about New Brighton apart from the fact that they had a professional football team in what was then known as the Third Division (North). I didn't even know that the Tower Ballroom, where we were to spend part of the evening, was once the tallest building in Britain. It is however a name that now rings huge bells in the memory, as will be seen in the next few paragraphs.

The first part of the evening was spent in a large pub close to the ballroom, where a sizeable number of us did Birkenhead Brewery's profits no harm at all. Somewhere round about the third pint we realised that we had either got Newton's twin brother with us, or the feared Drill Instructor of Flight3 Smuts Squadron had undergone a complete personality transplant. Was this guy, who was mixing freely with us and chatting away as though the past eight weeks hadn't existed, really the dreaded Newton, or was this some strange alcoholic hallucination? At that point we were past caring, and by 10 o'clock or thereabouts we had to apply what was left of our brains to the decision of what to do with the rest of the evening.

There were three choices. Half of the party went back to camp on one of the two civilian coaches, whilst the rest split between staying in the pub or heading for the dance at the nearby Tower Ballroom. I chose the dance option, but I have to say that my memories of it are very poor indeed. I remember the huge glass ball that rotated on the ceiling, a feature of most large dance halls at the time, and I remember coming down several flights of stone steps to the exit at the end.

As for the sight that confronted us as we stepped out into the night, I have no memory problems whatsoever with that.

Confronting us in a menacing semi-circle was an equal number of hard-looking locals. Obviously they were looking for a bit of 'blue uniform bashing', and we were on their territory. This was after all 1956. Large-scale battles at dance halls were commonplace, and we weren't the only ones in uniform. They were all kitted out in the teddy-boy gear of the time, and it seems strange looking back that serious punch-ups were always carried out in best suits.

They took us completely by surprise, and the initial rush was followed by a skirmish probably involving forty or fifty people right outside the dance hall. A certain amount of alcohol may well assist one's chances in a situation of this kind, but we were well past this stage and in danger of being completely overrun.

We managed to pull ourselves together enough to retreat, more or less as a group, to the top of some steps at the entrance to the car park. During a slight lull, where the action was more verbal than physical, we set about re-grouping and taking stock of the situation. Thankfully Newton had arrived on the scene by now and had assumed the role of battle commander. I don't think that this was an entirely new situation as far as he was concerned. He seemed in his element directing operations and playing a major part himself, as the two groups came together in a several spells of violent action before retreating to their 'bases' at the top and bottom of the steps

I devoted quite a few words to the ensuing battle when writing my 1967 version. Looking back, I wonder if the chance of a good story resulted in a bit of over dramatisation. However consultation with Sheff recently seems to knock that idea on the head. It was a perfectly good story without the need for any fictionalising. The time lapse wasn't a problem as I had my earlier notes to refer to. The problem is by how much did a massive collective amount of brown liquid distort the various versions.

I do know that I wandered about amongst the mayhem, contributing very little and surprisingly escaping injury. At one point I remember running back to our coach, on the other side of the car park, to try and enlist help from those that had not gone into the dance hall. This possibly was a touch optimistic. Having stayed in the pub until closing time, they were well past the 'fighting drunk' stage and well into 'sleeping drunk' mode.

My arrival at the coach may have caused the driver to have fears for the safety of his vehicle. Almost as soon as I had returned to the fray, we looked round to see the coach heading across the car park without us. The driver was only moving to a safer spot, but I think we had the idea that he was leaving us behind. Either way, this seemed to be the time for a strategic retreat, so we turned and made a run for it. There was a mad scramble to get aboard, and just as my turn came, something very heavy, thrown by one of the locals, hit the coach above me and dropped onto my head. I was bodily swept up the steps by the crowd behind, grazing my shins and ending up face down in the gangway.

We had some casualties, and it was obvious that as several of these were cuts of varying severity, some sort of weaponry had been involved. On arrival at West Kirby, the coach headed straight for the camp hospital, where seven of our number remained for several days. Since the passing out parade was only two days away, the unfortunate seven spent part of their post square bashing leave still at West Kirby.

Some time later I learned that Sheff, who I only knew in passing at that time, had been head-butted and had temporarily lost consciousness. As he felt himself being dragged to his feet, he thought he was in for another bashing, but was in fact being helped to safety by a passing civilian couple. His head was so badly bruised that he was unable to get his peaked cap on, and subsequently missed the passing-out parade for this reason.

I think we may have scored a few consolation points. There was a story that one of our blokes had picked up a large rock from the rockery at the top of the car park steps, and thrown it into the advancing 'enemy'. At the police enquiry the following morning, someone confirmed that one of the locals had suffered a broken collar bone. It later turned out that the whole affair was a bit of a hang over from a similar session the previous week, where the locals hadn't come out of it too well.

The great day finally arrived. The passing out parade was a very formal and ceremonious occasion, performed in front of a few parents and a line of important officers, with 'scrambled egg' very much in evidence. For the uninitiated, this is a reference to the gold braid on the peaked caps of highly ranked officers.

The parade passed without incident and we were really quite brilliant. Newton had done his job well. It was all over, or at least the West Kirby bit was. We were in no doubt that no other period in our two years service was going to be anything like these last two months. There were good and bad times, and I had it better than most, being able to escape to my running training every afternoon.

Newton dominated the whole two months. He did what he was paid to do; he wasn't there to be liked. He was there when we needed his leadership at New Brighton, and he probably changed our view of him on the results of that day alone. In the unlikely event of him reading this, I don't think he would be too unhappy at what I have said about him. I wonder where he is and what he did with the rest of his life, particularly after National Service came to an end a few years later.

After the parade we packed our kitbags and lined up outside of the billets in the usual formation, ready to be marched off by one of the lesser drill instructors. Newton stood in the doorway of one of the billets, a satisfied smile on his face. As we moved off one or two chanced their luck with a 'Cheerio Geordie'. We were relieved to see the smile remain. I suppose he had a Christian name. We never knew what it was.

I've never been back to West Kirby, and until I started this project I could not have pinpointed the camp location accurately on the map. Much of what I am writing comes from my earlier notes and from memory, but I am doing a small amount of research as I go along. I was pleased to discover that among a series of walks designed by Wirral Council, there is one that not only covers part of my old running area around Thurstaston Common, but also goes right through the camp.

The accompanying notes tell me that the buildings were demolished in 1986 and that a programme of tree planting commenced. Some of the old camp roads still exist, and the area is now a public open space. Wirral Council's notes relating to the camp finish with the invitation, 'Feel free to wander around this peaceful area'. One day I may do so, but I will be thinking of times when it wasn't quite so peaceful.

I also got quite excited when I spotted something on the map of the walk, which I thought was going to give me a perfect ending to this particular chapter. Believe it or not, the area of West Kirby closest to the camp is called Newton. This couldn't possibly be in honour of his services to the discipline of the Nation's youth, could it? Sadly no. Further research revealed that the parish of Newton was established rather earlier than Royal Air Force West Kirby.

Could anywhere look more bleak and uninviting than the Smuts Squadron parade ground in mid-winter?

West Kirby Drill Instructor Colin 'Geordie' Newton in the 1950s, and below receiving the British Empire Medal in 1969.

3. Sandwich

Having successfully negotiated the horrors of West Kirby, I entered the next phase of my service career with a new title. For the next four weeks I would be 2782765 AC2 Taylor RF. Radar Operator U/T (under training). It seemed that the RAF did not wish to make use of the skills that I had acquired during the three years of my apprenticeship, so I wasn't going to become an Airframe Mechanic, which was my first choice of trade. Perhaps they had a surplus of toolmakers and sheet metalworkers at this stage. I didn't get my second or third choice either, not that I can remember what they were. Radar Operator was my fourth selection, and I felt reasonably happy to settle for that.

I had a rail warrant from West Kirby to the opposite corner of the country, where my training was to take place at RAF Sandwich in Kent. The warrant allowed for a break in the journey at Welwyn Garden City, as there was a leave period between square bashing and trade training. I wasn't sure how a week at home would work out, and although it was to prove fairly uneventful, it was to influence events that happened a few weeks later at Easter.

I ran in one cross-country event for the club in this period but couldn't escape from the Air Force even at home. The run was at Luton, against the home club and RAF Halton, who had two decent runners in sergeants Danny Gallagher and Don Cobley, who were first and third, with Harry Wilson from our club in between. Although I had been performing well in service events, I was all over the place at home, finishing well down the field in this one. This was my tenth race in as many weeks, which today would be considered a bit over the top for an 18-year-old.

With the leave over, a small group assembled at Charing Cross Station bound for the historic Cinque Port of Sandwich. The town now lies two miles inland, but the River Stour is still navigable to certain vessels over a five-mile winding course from Pegwell Bay. I must however resist the temptation to stray from the original purpose of this exercise and remember that this is not a travel guide. The historic delights of Sandwich are many, but are well documented elsewhere.

The sight that confronted us at the gates of Royal Air Force Sandwich however was pure 1950s. The place was alive with 'bull'. Everywhere we looked people were scrubbing and painting things. In the middle of the road men were furiously scrubbing at oil patches, all ropes in view were being white painted, steps were being red polished, windows were being cleaned. In fact everything was being cleaned.

Our spirits sank. We thought that we had left all of this behind at West Kirby. As we lined up in the Station Warrant Officers room to await instructions there were a lot of long faces and a general air of depression.

The gloom lifted quickly when we discovered that, apart from one of our number who was required at Sandwich as an accounts clerk, we were all due for onward shipment along the coast to a smaller camp at St. Margaret's Bay. This was where the four-week radar course was to take place. As Sandwich was the parent unit, it was deemed necessary to send us there first for admin purposes.

The SWO located the papers for the rest of the group, but after a lengthy search could find no record of anything relating to a certain AC2 Taylor. The other half dozen or so were quickly despatched to St Margaret's while I remained in the office awaiting decision. My unaccounted for presence was causing a surprising amount of disturbance. I was soon to find out why and also to learn the reason for the astonishing amount of 'bull' going on outside.

After much telephoning the SWO admitted that there had been a cock-up somewhere and as far as he was concerned I didn't exist. 'The Duchess of Gloucester is inspecting this camp tomorrow,' he said, half in despair and half in anger. 'I've got everyone accounted for. I know where they will be and what they will be doing. I can't afford to have any spare bods around with nothing to do. I want you off this camp by nine o'clock tomorrow morning. And I don't want to see you back until after seven o'clock in the evening.'

With that he drew six bob from petty cash for 'out of camp meals expenses', thereby earning himself a twenty-four-hour reprieve in his efforts to sort out the strange case of AC2 Taylor.

The accounts clerk and I drew some bedding, but found a problem in finding somewhere to put it. There were no spare beds in any of the billets for either of us, even though he was due to be part of the Sandwich personnel. Two beds were temporarily set up in an annexe behind one of the billets, so I made up mine and started to consider what to do with ten hours and six bob the following day.

By nine o'clock I was off the camp and into the town at Sandwich. After killing an hour or so in a café and a quick look round the town, I headed towards the outskirts, on the Canterbury road. I was about to have my first attempt at the National Serviceman's preferred form of transport, the art of lift thumbing. The risks to a driver or a passenger attached to this exercise nowadays are too serious to contemplate, but in the 1950s it was a common and generally safe practice. National Servicemen didn't have the sort of money to cover train fares home on a regular basis, so some journeys were willingly subsidised by lorry drivers or private motorists. Generally speaking, a young person with a holdall, standing by the side of a busy road thumbing a lift, was more often than not a serviceman trying to get home. Drivers in the main recognised this and were very cooperative.

My first effort was an instant success, and I was in Canterbury in no time. With plenty to choose from, I opted for an hour in the cathedral before pressing on and arriving in Maidstone, courtesy of another generous driver. After a brief inspection of Maidstone town centre, another lift saw me back in Canterbury for tea, followed by a bus back to Sandwich as it was now dark. A leisurely pint killed off a bit of spare time, and I was back in the fold shortly after eight. An unusual but not unpleasant day.

The following day the Station Warrant Officer had come no nearer to solving my problem. In fairness, he probably had quite enough to worry about with the VIP visit. It was generally a case of stay on the camp and someone will find you if we hear anything. I had already spotted a sports field with a respectable grass running track marked out, plus some decent changing rooms. I was surprised to see the track, since it was March and a long time since the previous summer's track season. I was to learn later that athletics was a priority sport on the camp, due mainly to the efforts of one very enthusiastic officer.

Out came the running gear. I got in a decent session of an hour or so in the morning and in the absence of anything better to do, another one in the afternoon. I felt that I could get used to this. If nobody rumbled me, my form could improve dramatically.

Later that afternoon my accounts buddy was moved into a billet and with him went his alarm clock, my only means of telling the time.

Next morning I woke up, alone in the annexe, without knowing whether it was breakfast time or teatime. I dressed quickly and went to the door of the annexe to seek assistance, but my problems were resolved immediately with the striking of the church clock, which I could just see registering eight o'clock between the trees.

After breakfast I pottered down to the office to see if I had finally become a statistic on the SWO's records, but again the results were negative. Out came the running kit again for a third training session in the space of not much more than 24 hours.

During this session I met one of the stars of the camp team, Mike Soames, whose civilian club was Essex Beagles. Mike was the Essex Junior 440yds champion with a best time of around 51secs. From him I learned that in the summer the camp fielded a decent track and field team, with enough athletes to cover the full programme of events for matches against the local clubs. The most prominent member of the team was the long jumper John Lissaman of Blackheath Harriers, who four years later ranked fourth in the country at his event.

The driving force behind the team was Flight Lieutenant Jim Chadwin, who wasn't just responsible for the administration as is often the case with service sports teams. He was an extremely active and enthusiastic member of the team, being prepared to fill in at any event from sprints to steeplechase. He also managed a good shot at being one of the blokes without losing the respect his rank commanded. His favourite event was 440yards hurdles, and he finished second in the Kent Championships that year.

Later that day I was called to the Station Warrant Officer's office to be told that they had finally solved the mystery of what to do with me. Guess what, I should have gone to St. Margaret's with the others three days ago. Now there's a surprise! I was three days behind on the course but I had managed to get in three unexpected training sessions and had a day out in Canterbury and Maidstone. I had also made contact with the Sandwich athletics team, which was to prove useful later on, so it wasn't all bad!

4.   St. Margaret's

I did my initial radar training in a small village approximately twenty miles from Calais, but had no need of a French phrase book. St. Margaret's Bay is as near as you can get to France without getting your feet wet, and has been the traditional starting or finishing point for cross channel swimmers since Captain Webb's first successful crossing in 1875.

Strictly speaking the course was at St. Margaret's at Cliffe, which is a further mile or so inland and, according to most maps, a separate village altogether. The names are however a true description. One is mainly either halfway down or at the bottom of the cliff, while the other is entirely at the top.

I arrived there on Thursday evening, after three days of being a displaced person at Sandwich, to link up with the rest of the course, who had arrived on the Monday. There were twenty of us spread over two billets, with five to a room. The accommodation was vastly different to West Kirby, with radiators, tiled floors, and a separate room containing all of the usual offices within the billet.

There was one empty bed, which I obviously should have been in three days earlier, in a room where I recognised three of the other four occupants. John Parker, from Bedford, had been in my billet on the first week at Cardington, while Les Willmore, from Ilford, was with me at West Kirby. John Shefford, from central London, had been in the next billet at both camps. Apart from a four-month spell later that year 'Sheff' was to occupy the same billet as me for the rest of our service. Only Brian Howard from Harrow was a completely new face.

Among the other members of the course were Derek Henry from Catford, who was to remain at St. Margaret's with me after the training was finished; Geoff Clamp, a pot-holer from Derbyshire (where else!); Fred Ketteridge from Bishop's Stortford, who was unusual in that he was a car-owner; Harry Harris from Lincoln; and Trevor Fox from Barnsley.

Brian Howard at the time was following Nevil Shute's *Beyond the Black Stump* which was being serialised in the *John Bull* magazine and which he passed on to me afterwards. As a result, I can see all twenty-three of Nevil Shute's books from where I sit, although I haven't read any of them for many years. Perhaps I should start again and see if I enjoy them as much as I did forty years ago.

The following day I met our Instructor, Chief Technician Youll, a fairly portly, fiftyish family man who had a lengthy service history. The story was that he had been demobbed once and secured a good position with Decca, but was unable to settle and returned to the Air Force within six months. I have no means of knowing if this is correct, but this was the story on the camp at the time.

Chief-Tech Youll was a radar encyclopaedia. The radar system that we were being trained on was called CH (Chain Home), the earliest form of radar, that was used to good effect in World War 2, most notably during the Battle of Britain. It was, however, to become obsolete about three months after our course finished. Our instructor poured out facts at an astonishing rate, writing them on the blackboard at the same time. We had to write it all into notebooks at such a speed there was no time to digest any of the information. I don't remember understanding it then, so I am certainly not in a position to elaborate on any of it now. During my service time I was employed on three different types of radar, but can only recall the most basic of details from any of them. There are, however, many people intensely interested in radar history with available information growing all of the time, particularly on the Internet.

I don't seem to have quite the same difficulty remembering where all of the pubs were. All camps had a NAAFI where it was possible to buy a fair variety of drink, but apart from Barkway, my next station, they were a bit short on atmosphere. It was generally considered better to have evenings out in the local inns. At St. Margaret's at Cliffe there were three pubs plus a café called The Quality Inn. We tended to favour the nearest one to the camp, The Hope. On our first visit we noticed a chair in the corner of the Public Bar, which had an engraved label carrying the words Devils Corner. We learned that this was the usual seat of the St Margaret's

Station Warrant Officer, Sergeant 'Dusty' Miller, who was a very valuable and regular customer.

Sergeant 'Dusty' was a serious football man who ran the camp team and was always on the lookout for new recruits to strengthen the squad. All newcomers, after passing the guardroom, had to report to the SWO for checking in and billet allocation, etc. His first words to all new arrivals were 'Do you play football?' I said that I did and was still partial to the occasional game, but explained the athletics situation, which he readily accepted.

This is straying off the previous subject of pubs and their locations. Our next discovery was a tiny pub in the equally tiny village of Martin Mill, two miles away. Tiny though it was, the village had a railway station, which was the nearest one to the camp and from which we had to walk in the early hours of the morning when returning from a 48hr pass or leave. The pub was miniscule, with just one bar no more than ten feet square that accommodated about a dozen people comfortably. We found it very agreeable, and as the weather got better it was quite an acceptable walk.

Later on, when the course was finished and I became part of the permanent staff at St. Margaret's, I was included in demob parties, which were usually held in yet another pub, The Green Man, in an unusual setting right on the edge of the beach. The pub was reached from a long winding road, descending some 250feet. But the distance, if not the descent, could be shortened by 200 steps which cut out the bend in the road. The route back, involving 200yards uphill before and after the steps, provided a fitting finale to the evening's entertainment.

I kept my athletics training going on the camp football pitch, around the local lanes and along grassy paths on the cliff top. I was pleased to find an occasional training companion in Arthur Stainer of Camberley Athletic Club, who was a notch or two above my standard. I remembered seeing his name in *Athletics Weekly* before Christmas, when he had finished 18th in the South of the Thames Cross Country Championship. I had been 83rd in the corresponding North of the Thames race. We, however, were not the only two athletes in regular training, as there was another in the unlikely form of Percy Henry. I say unlikely, because anyone not in the know who had observed Percy in his day-to-day movements about the camp, would have been astonished at the transformation once he had a pair of spiked shoes on his feet. Percy was never in a hurry, sauntering to and fro about the camp at a speed marginally above nought miles per hour, so I was more than a bit surprised when he turned up at the sports field in a tracksuit and carrying a pair of running spikes.

He wasn't a great communicator, but I learned that he was a member of the London club Polytechnic Harriers, at that time one of the top clubs in the country, with times of around 10.1secs for 100 yards and 50.5secs for 440yds to his credit. Once I saw him in action, I had no doubt about the authenticity of these times.

Very early in my time at St. Margaret's the Easter holiday arrived. I expected to go home, but a telegram from my stepmother telling me not to go forced a quick change of plan. The following day a long rambling letter arrived. I was being informed that the family budget could not fund regular visits from a non-paying guest. I had recently been home for a week at the end of square bashing and with no spare money whatsoever had not offered any contribution to my keep. This had obviously led to problems that I had been unaware of. There were many other deep-rooted factors, and the tone of the letter indicated that it was not just Easter when I wouldn't be welcome. In a normal family situation, this sort of thing could have been resolved with a short discussion, but I wasn't part of a normal situation.

Up to this stage I have been having mixed feelings about how much detail I should include relating to my home situation. I am writing a detailed account of a two-year period of my life, with the main theme being a description of my spell of National Service. Inevitably a large amount of athletics detail has come into the story, as athletics featured very prominently in my life and continued to do so after my service time finished. On the same basis my home situation influenced much of my thinking and was relevant to much of what was happening, at least for most of the first year, so it seems impossible to omit it from the story as a whole. After the first year it became less important, as will be seen as things progress.

The Easter business led to me not going home for a long period. Eventually I wrote several times to ask if it was convenient to come home and when none of my letters were answered, I finally wrote to my father at his work address. He wrote a brief note back to say to come home, but I had obviously put him in a difficult position, and I am not at all sure how he squared this with my step-mother. After this I went home at very infrequent intervals, slept on the settee and was always careful to pay my way. In the intervening period I went to Welwyn Garden City several times, even if I didn't go home. I stayed with friends a couple of times, but also had weekends where I slept on Welwyn Garden City station, Dover station, and in the boys' club.

While the radar course was in progress, things were not so bad, as several others on the course didn't go home all that often. Once the course was over and the members were dispersed to various other radar stations, the situation changed. I was to remain at St. Margaret's. It seemed then that most of the camp went home at weekends, and those that didn't were on duty. Consequently I spent quite a few lonely weekends roaming around St. Margaret's Bay and further afield in Dover, Deal, and even Folkestone. Strangely on two visits to Folkestone I bumped into people from Hertfordshire, on holiday. First was a runner from Watford called Johnson with his family; the other was a former workmate Keith Hartridge and his girlfriend, who oddly enough I had been instrumental in bringing together.

This generally was a fairly depressing period, which was to last until September, when a change of camp brought about a different set of circumstances. It took three years before relations at home improved. In the first eighteen months after demob from the Air Force, I cannot remember any contact at all, but things did eventually straighten out. My stepmother and my father came to my wedding and were very generous with their present. My father died before my three daughters were born, but my stepmother lived for a further sixteen years and did her best to play her part in mending the bridges and to become a grandmother to my daughters.

All of this is well in the past and depressing to recall, but the memories are always there, just below the surface. I have, however tried to kill it all off in one go, with the hope that I will not need to refer to it again for the rest of the story.

Back with the radar lessons and several note-books-full later, the course finally ground to its conclusion, and the very pleasant Chief-Tech Youll vanished from our lives. The next step was to pair us all up and despatch us to various radar sites around the coast. Derek Henry and I were despatched a mere 100 yards across the camp, as we had come out of the hat as the two people needed to supplement the RAF St. Margaret's staff.

Completion of the course brought about my promotion to Aircraftsman 1 (AC1), but more important, was a forty-six per cent increase from twenty-four bob per week to thirty-five bob, or £1.75 to those not conversant with medieval finance.

The eight other occupants of our new billet were all employed on a different type of radar to the course that Derek and I had just completed. They were all Radar Operators (PPI), while we were Radar Operators (CH). For them, the working day was spent 60 feet underground as part of the Rotor chain of radar stations that had been built around Britain's coastline in the early 1950s. The Chain Home system was an entirely above-ground operation.

The three other members of the room to which Derek and I had been consigned were, Roy Dodson from Wembley, Brian Williamson from Oxford, and John 'Chips' Hurd from Mottingham. No, this isn't a typing error. I didn't know that there was a place called Mottingham either.

Williamson, a former rugby player, was on light duties following a back injury and very close to a medical discharge. John Hurd is going to occupy a few more lines. A Scotsman, originally from the Isle of Mull, he claimed to be a relation of the actress Thora Hird, despite the difference in the spelling of the surnames, and he patriotically wore his kilt on off-duty periods. He was usually last out of bed on duty mornings, assisted by a dose of traditional Scottish medicine before his feet hit the floor and was last aboard the truck to the radar site. I wonder perhaps if I had gone a little bit over the top when I made my 1967 attempt on these memoirs, as my notes had him listed as a Kent fencing champion, leader of the local Scout troop and a proficient enough bagpipe player to be an instructor to The Deal Girl Pipers! I would be really pleased for him to read this and tell me if I've got it right.

The billet was a two-roomed affair with the other room housing an interesting mixture. Brian Pinnock was a big barn door type full-back, who was captain of the camp football team. In civilian life he played at good quality non-league level for Enfield Town. He and his mate Terry Saunders from nearby Folkestone were very close to demob and counting the days. Ernie Frith was another near local, from Sittingbourne. Although classified as a radar operator, his chief occupation while on duty was to man the tea-bar at the underground radar site. Ron Benbow from Hammersmith, who was later posted to Northern Ireland and Tony Phoenix from Harrow made up the five.

I hadn't been in this billet very long, when one weekend I found myself the only resident. The other nine had gone home and were not due back until one or two o'clock on Monday morning. I had gone to bed around eleven on the Sunday and about an hour later woke up with a start as I felt someone touch me. After the initial panic had subsided, I realised that it was Sergeant Dusty Miller, a little worse for wear after a heavy evening in The Hope. He leaned over me and said, 'Where's that skiving bugger Williamson?' referring to the rugby player on light duties. I said, 'He's not back from 48 yet Sarge.' Whereupon he uttered a few oaths and went out, slamming the doors on the way. I had no idea what he wanted with Williamson at midnight on a Sunday. Williamson was none the wiser when I recounted the story in slightly modified form the next morning.

I was now ready to start duty as a CH operator. We were ferried out to the two radar sites by truck, the CH operators going West towards Dover, the others to the underground site just to the East of the village, but nearer to the cliff edge than our site. The CH operation was at an area called Swingate, where the site comprised the radar block and a small guardroom. The only living accommodation was a caravan in which one of the officers and his wife lived.

RAF Swingate figures prominently in Airforce folklore, having been a Royal Flying Corps airfield in World War1. It was also a fully staffed camp in World War 2, seeing considerable action at its exposed and dangerous location on the top of the cliffs. The CH radar operation commenced at Swingate in 1938 when the massive 350 feet towers were built. They are still in use today for various communication purposes, having become a famous landmark over the years. Being clearly visible from the French coast, they were a frequent wartime target. Arriving three days late for the CH course, after my escapade at Sandwich, I probably missed any historical detail that Chief-Tech Youll may have imparted concerning the Swingate site. Airmen and WAAFs who had lost their lives in bombing raids just 12 years earlier, had operated the same equipment in the same buildings. I was quite unaware of so serious a connection at the time.

The towers will always be remembered by a certain former AC1 Taylor, not so much for events that happened in 1956, but for a much more recent event, 1994 to be precise. On a weekend break in the Canterbury area with my wife and youngest daughter, I caught sight of the towers through the battlements, while on a visit to Dover Castle. Feeling a surge of nostalgia, I rushed over for a closer look and slipped on the wet paving, doing the back of my head some serious damage as it came second in an argument with a very solid cannon.

While my daughter did her best to keep the blood on the inside of my head, my wife ran for help. English Heritage swung into action and rushed the three of us to Dover Hospital in a Land Rover. I then had two stitches in the back of my head, without anaesthetic or any other form of painkiller. The nurse said, 'This is going to make your toes curl.' And she wasn't wrong. English Heritage came back to collect us and take us back to the Castle and with my head bound up in a large turban we continued our day out.

The watch at Swingate consisted of about six of us, including Percy the sprinter and Keith Girling from Bristol, but the others have vanished completely from the memory bank. We were under the supervision of one of the four WAAF officers on the camp,

Pilot Officer Hopkins. Although no older than the others on the watch, she probably had more brains than the rest of us put together, and as far as I can remember managed things most efficiently. She always seemed slightly embarrassed by the authority that she carried, but she was generally very agreeable, in more ways than one. She was often to be seen carrying armfuls of books about the camp. We took great pleasure in saluting her and watching her struggle to return the salute without spilling books all over the road. All very juvenile! To her credit, she took it all in good spirit, which only serves to confirm her status in relation to the miserable 'erks' under her supervision.

I made arrangements for the newsagent in the village to order my *Athletics Weekly* and was surprised to learn that someone on the camp called Holt had made the same arrangement. I thought that the number of practising athletes at St. Margaret's only totalled three, although another was to be posted in very soon and two more came out of the closet at the station sports day in July.

It didn't take me long to find Mike Holt from Maidstone. (How did all these Kent people manage to get a posting so close to home?) We were paired together on guard duty at the Swingate radar site, and it transpired that he was a very rare specimen for 1956. He was a jogger. Today, thanks to the vision of the late Chris Brasher and his marvellous brainchild The London Marathon, the country is awash with joggers, and there is a competitive outlet for all abilities. Running is now a sport for the masses, instead of just the talented few, with all of the resultant health benefits. There are now far more joggers than serious club athletes, but this was not the case in the 1950s and 1960s. Anyone who ran then was a serious club athlete. Athletic clubs did very little to encourage anyone who didn't meet the generally accepted minimum standard, and those who ran outside of the club system were very rare indeed. I remember seeing a bus conductor wearing trainers on the Isle of Wight in the late 1960s. I assumed that he was an athlete and asked him which club he ran for. I hadn't expected to receive any other answer than that of an athletic club, and I wasn't disappointed.

Mike was a very keen runner and interested in the sport as a whole, but unfortunately not quite up to club standard. I hope that he carried on. He would be O.K. today among us old stagers still trying to maintain a competitive urge. He was however the right person for me to share a guard duty with. It was a guard duty that passed without incident until 2am, when we were required to unlock the gate to let in the car containing the officer and his wife who lived in the caravan on the site. Our duty didn't stop there, as we then had to help get the officer, who had obviously had a very good evening in the Officers' Mess, into the caravan.

The following morning there was a tradition to be upheld. It was a custom for those on guard duty to climb one of the radar towers for as far as their nerve held out. It was said that the view was magnificent, but I would be very surprised if anyone reached anywhere near the total height of around 350 feet. I am sorry to say that with a fair wind blowing, even at ground level, I declined Mike Holt's invitation to have 'a little climb', watching from the guardroom as his sanity returned fairly early into his ascent.

Shortly afterwards, the CH (Chain Home) radar was rendered obsolete, having served its purpose, and the watch was discontinued. It is possible that I was on the last ever watch at this famous station. The few of us on this type of radar were quickly retrained as PPI Operators to work on the Centrimetric Early Warning system, 'down the hole', as the underground site was generally referred to.

At the end of May I watched the Kent Athletics Championships at the Crabble Ground in Dover, which gave me the idea of joining Dover Athletic Club, since it seemed that I had now got a permanent posting in the area. The following Sunday morning I put on my kit and ran the four miles or so along the coast road, past the Bleriot memorial and the castle, and into the town to the Crabble Ground.

When I arrived there was not a soul in sight, which I thought strange since athletic clubs throughout the country meet on Sunday mornings. I didn't know then that the ground was used as a secondary venue to Canterbury for Kent county cricket matches.

Despite the official title of Crabble Athletic Ground, the chances of the local athletic club being able to use it were very slim indeed.

I ran back to camp and next time in Dover made enquiries at the local library. Their information was a bit out of date. After finding Major Petrie, who the library informed me was the secretary, he told me that he was no longer in office. The current secretary was also the club's best distance runner, Doug Penn, but Major Petrie did not know his address. He did know, however, that members of his family ran a fish and chip shop in London Road, which was now step three in my efforts to join Dover Athletic Club. By chance Doug Penn called in while I was in the shop, so I signed up and for all that effort got to run in just one competition for Dover, an inter club match at Hythe against the local club and Maidstone Athletic Club.

Doug told me that the club met on Sundays at a recreation ground in the town. I ran over a couple of times from the camp, on one occasion meeting my first coal-miner. No, he wasn't from Barnsley or Merthyr Tydfill. He was a nineteen-year-old discus thrower from Dover who worked down a mine right there in Kent in the Garden of England.

I was aware that there were coalmines in Kent. Alan Tapson, who was in my billet at West Kirby, came from Aylesham which was close to Snowdown Colliery. Later on, when I was making bus trips to Sandwich for athletic events, the bus from Dover and Deal passed close to the mines at Tillmanstone and Betteshanger. Although I knew that they were there, I was still unprepared for the sight of coal mining machinery sticking up into the Kent countryside.

With the others on the CH course scattered around radar sites in various parts of the country, Derek Henry and I had been a bit isolated from the other St. Margaret's inmates up to the time that the Swingate site ceased to function. Not only were we on a different type of radar to the rest of the billet while the CH system was still running, we were considerably newer in terms of service and didn't fit readily into any particular group. We tended therefore to spend a fair bit of time together during the weekday off-duty periods and became quite good mates. I have kept contact with four former colleagues from a later period of my service, but Derek and I lost touch after we were both moved on from St. Margaret's, but in different directions.

Back in the middle of 1956, however, we were virtually a two man expeditionary force, with a mission to examine as many public houses as possible in the Dover and Deal area. We found a decent one in Dover, which boasted a television set, a considerable rarity in those days, while further exploration unearthed others in the neighbouring villages of Ringwould and Kingsdown. One evening, in Deal we found a pub that was very much to our liking, so much so that we missed the last bus back to St. Margaret's. Since it was a ruling at the time that anyone under twenty-one had to be back on camp by midnight during the week, this gave us less than an hour and a half to cover somewhere between five and six miles by alternative means. If we couldn't get a lift, which seemed unlikely in our present state, and in the dark, then it would have to be on foot.

We set off in reasonable spirits making quite good progress with alternate spells of walking and what might be termed 'alcoholic sprinting', attempting to thumb a lift every now and then. It seemed that we were not wrong in our assessment of how difficult it would be to get a lift. The public generosity that was usually displayed on Friday and Sunday evenings didn't extend to this type of scenario, so we resigned ourselves to carry on with plan B. We knew that we had to take a left turn off the Deal to Dover road, but we didn't know where it was, or how far it was. It meant that every road sign at left turns had to be very carefully inspected, which was not easy in the dark and with little help from car headlights.

The fresh air coupled with the urgency of the situation sobered us up very quickly. Eventually we made it back to the camp in good time but not without a few anxious moments. As relative newcomers on the camp, we hadn't yet discovered the alternative way in through the back fence, which would have taken some of the stress out of the occasion.

A very large percentage of our 35-bob pay was spent on Thursday evenings, pay parade having been earlier in the day, with most of the rest going over the weekend. If we could survive to

Tuesday, we then had the chance of some additional earnings. Tuesday night was 'bull-night', when everything had to be made ready for the Wednesday morning inspection and we had a standing order to press the trousers of the demob-happy Brian Pinnock and Terry Saunders. Both were revelling in the comparative affluence of seventy-six bob (£3.80) per week, the standard pay for a senior aircraftsman in the last six months of service. We charged half a crown each (twelve and a half pence) but should have increased the price for Brian Pinnock, as he was a very large bloke indeed! His trousers were probably all of fifty per cent larger than Terry's.

On Wednesday evening we pooled our resources, and if we could rake up the 1956 equivalent of about 4p.each, we could treat ourselves to a plate of chips and baked beans, and a cup of tea in the NAAFI.

Between the radar duties and the evening revelry, I was continuing to train fairly regularly, but not getting the amount of races that I would have liked. In 1955 as a junior (under 19), I had taken part in 32 track races, but this year I had to make do with half of that number. I had three races in Hertfordshire, the only one of significance being a good quality junior half-mile race at Watford, where I improved my personal best time to 2mins 5.6secs. In 1955 a time of 2mins 11secs had been good enough to get me into the final, but this time I didn't survive the heats. For all of these races I hitch-hiked the whole way to Welwyn Garden City and also back as far as London, but then caught the last train from Charing Cross back to Martin Mill, along with several others. Occasionally we would be met by a truck, but even with that assistance it was 1.30 or thereabouts before we arrived back at camp.

The chance of some additional races came courtesy of Flight Lieutenant Jim Chadwin at Sandwich, who invited Arthur Stainer, Percy Henry and me to take part in their station championships. There was no one in the Sandwich team to match Percy at the 100 and 220 yards, and he won both sprints with ease. Arthur and I however came up against a very powerful runner called Jim Pierce in the one and three mile events. The order was the same in both races, Pierce, Arthur and then me. Jim Chadwin was sufficiently impressed to include us in the Sandwich team for two matches against the local club, Thanet A.C., one at Sandwich and one at Broadstairs.

The next item on the agenda was the No.11 Group Championships at the RAF Stadium at Uxbridge. Here I got the thin end of the wedge, as only one runner was permitted for each event. With Pierce taking the mile and Arthur the three miles, I went along as reserve only. Had I been on most other stations in the group I would have got a run; indeed in the following year's No. 11 Group championship I finished second in the three miles. In consolation, it did mean a whole week away from duties, as we trained for three days at Sandwich before spending two days at the championships. We travelled to Uxbridge by coach, stopping at a large café at Gillingham en route. The café had a large supply of mugs on which were printed in red 'Stolen from the Pavilion Café Gillingham' or whatever the name was. This made them very attractive to the female members of the team, who were carrying zip-up shoulder bags, with the result that the mugs were very much in evidence in the Sandwich cookhouse the following week.

Back at St. Margaret's, my ranking dropped even further with the arrival on the camp of Derek Smith of Bristol Athletic Club, the Gloucestershire Junior Cross Country Champion. Derek added a bit of spice to our training runs, since he was even a notch ahead of Arthur. I was now faced with the situation where at West Kirby, among 3000 plus recruits, I could come second in the cross country championship, yet here on a camp of around two hundred bodies I was only third in the pecking order.

In normal circumstances this would not have been a problem, but the authorities at St Margaret's decided, probably for the first time ever, to hold a station sports day. On any other camp of 200 personnel, I ought to have been able to bank on at least one success at either half-mile or one mile, possibly both. At St. Margaret's I couldn't even hope for a second place in either. If Percy decided to do the quarter-mile as well as the two shorter sprints, I had no chance of success at all. If not, then I might just sneak a win at the shorter distance and avoid total disgrace.

In the end I hedged my bets and entered the 440 yards (quarter mile) and the mile and hoped that Arthur was not having similar thoughts. As it happened Percy wasn't feeling energetic enough to tackle the quarter, while Arthur hadn't been devious enough to even consider it. For my sins I had to run a heat and final, but won both, for which I received a fairly elegant cruet set, which served the Taylor household well for about ten years. I also ran the mile, coming third behind Derek and Arthur with Mike Holt fourth, who probably also felt pretty aggrieved to find the three of us on so small a station.

In all the sports day was a great success and brought forth a couple of surprises in the form of ex-athletes, neither of whom I had any idea had been connected with the sport. The PBX operator emerged from behind his switchboard in the colours of Essex club Hadleigh Olympiades and ran second to Percy in the 100 and 220 yards, while the red and black hoops of Herne Hill Harriers were stretched around the ample frame of Radar Mechanic Mike Locke, who proved a more than capable javelin winner. Both sets of kit vanished into respective lockers after the sports day. They may have been pressed back into service after demob, but I certainly didn't see them in use again at St. Margaret's.

The highlight of the day came with the last event. Someone had the surprising foresight to put Percy's sprinting ability to maximum use, by setting up a two-man 100yards race between Percy and the No.1 speed man from the US Air Force base at nearby Manston. Amid wild excitement Percy got home by a couple of yards, before slipping back into casual mode and sauntering off to his billet to get changed.

With the solitary run that I managed for Dover Athletic Club, this was the sum total of my 1956 track season. I had managed to improve my times from last year, but not as much as I had hoped and was generally disappointed with the season as a whole.

With the closure of the CH radar, and our transfer to the underground operation, Derek and I were now part of a very different set-up indeed. In what is now referred to as The Cold War Period, a large number of underground installations were constructed along the south and east coasts in 1951 and 1952. The layout of these sites around the coast was similar, although some were on more than one level and not all operated the same type of radar. At St. Margaret's, the radar type was Centrimetric Early Warning. The operations rooms were reached through a bungalow-style guardroom, that was designed as a standard residential building to confuse the enemy. How the huge rotating aerial and nodding height-finding aerials nearby were supposed to fit into the domestic picture I am not at all sure.

Once we entered the guardroom, the next stage was through large steel doors, down a flight of steps and into a highly polished, gradually descending corridor about eight feet square and around 100 yards long. The estimates of the length of the corridor varied, depending on who was polishing it! Before entering the corridor, we changed our working boots for regulation black RAF plimsolls to protect the floor. At the end of the corridor, a left turn led through double doors into a smaller corridor, off of which were the main operations room, equipment rooms, plus rest room, kitchen and toilets.

I do remember a little more about the workings of this particular type of radar compared to the previous CH type. Without going too overboard on detail, the equipment was capable, with the assistance of the above ground moving aerials, of plotting approaching aircraft up to a range of 300 miles. It was possible to determine the direction, speed, height and even roughly how many aircraft might be in a particular group. Obviously with the rapid developments in the aircraft industry in the fifties, 300 miles was not going to remain satisfactory for very long, and indeed even this type of radar was coming to the end of its life during the latter part of my service period.

We worked in units of one hour on and one hour off, with the latter being far more taxing than the former. In these periods we were required, after a quick sit-down in the rest room and a cup of tea courtesy of Ernie Frith, to clean everything in sight every day, including one very long corridor. At least for this we had an electric polisher, which was run from power points spaced at intervals along the corridor. On one occasion, I was polishing the corridor entirely on my own, when in an attempt to gain the maximum area before changing power points, I pulled the wires out of the plug. I sat down on the floor and proceeded to reinstate the wires, using my dinner knife as a screwdriver. Completely engrossed in my DIY electrics, I failed to hear the approaching footsteps until they were almost upon me. I scrambled to my feet hurriedly, as half a dozen officers with a generous amount of gold braid between them swept by without a word.

I was told afterwards that it was a delegation of officers from the Swedish Air Force on a knowledge exchange visit. I have no means of knowing if this was true, but if this was the case, I don't think that I made a positive contribution to the British effort.

The number of personnel required for each watch was considerably more than that needed for the CH system. Not only were there a far greater range of operations to cover, three officers were required to supervise each watch. A Radar Controller, usually an officer of around Flight Lieutenant standing, was supported by two officers of lesser rank. The officer in charge of my watch, Flight Lieutenant Paton, was a tough officer who had reputedly risen through the ranks to attain officer status. The supporting roles were taken by two of the four female officers at St. Margaret's, Flight Officers Ness and Deuxchamps. Ness was short, slim and smart, and fairly fierce, while Deuxchamps, who I think was Belgian, was the exact opposite. When she was out of uniform it was unlikely that anyone could have guessed her role in life.

Only once during my spell at St. Margaret's was I caught for guard duty at the underground site. Dave Grimwade from Sheerness, - yes, another one of the Kent contingent, - was my colleague for this duty. This site however was considered rather more important than the CH Site, and warranted a military policeman plus a very large Alsatian in addition to the two of us. We were ferried to the site in the back of a small van, with the Alsatian a bit too close for my liking.

The duties were none too strenuous. Each hour Dave Grimwade and I did a tour of the perimeter fence, probably about half a mile, which on a warm summer evening up on top of the cliffs was not unpleasant. For the rest of the time up to midnight I spent the time sewing. Yes, sewing, and not just darning my socks! This obviously will need some explaining. In the 1950s, it was common practice for athletes to have the name of their club across the back of their tracksuit top at shoulder level. The larger clubs probably bought suits in bulk, with the name already printed. In smaller clubs like mine, athletes sported tracksuits of varying colours and put the name on the back themselves by whatever means available.

I was still wearing my first tracksuit, which was bottle green, so I had bought some yellow felt and used the guard period to cut out and sew on the letters. Luckily Welwyn A.C. only needed eight letters. It could have been worse, I could have been a member of Middlesbrough and Cleveland Harriers!

After midnight, guard duty took on a rather different complexion. Either Dave or I had to spend the rest of the night alone, 'down the hole', among the operations rooms and a long way from the others. I drew the short straw. The steel doors clanged shut behind me and I felt very alone as I set off down the seemingly endless tunnel, armed with a rifle, but thankfully no ammunition.

I had a quick look in the main operations room, which looked very sinister in the dark, and withdrew quickly to the rest room. Guard duty was putting it fairly loosely, since the rest room housed a camp bed, mattress and blankets. It was a bit frightening down there in the dark, although a comforting strip of light from the corridor showed below the rest room door. The other two were a long way away up in the guardroom, on the other side of very thick steel doors.

Surprisingly, I slept well up to about 6am, down there in the dark in the bowels of the earth. At 6am, I woke suddenly as the door opened, lighting up the corner of the rest room, before it was quickly closed again. A shadowy figure walked past the end of my bed and into the toilet, put the light on, had a pee, put the light off, came back past my bed and out of the door. Not a word was spoken on either side. I certainly didn't sleep after that. Should I have challenged him? (I assumed that it was a him; the ablutions sounded masculine.) The RAF would certainly have said yes, most of my colleagues probably would have said no. I readily admit to being scared stiff, and the guy was past my bed before I could get my head around the situation. Calling out 'Halt, who goes there?' from a position tucked up in bed, just as he was entering the loo, somehow seemed inappropriate. I had no warning that anyone else would be down there between midnight and 7am, when I was due to return to the guardroom. Later I found out that my visitor was not a spy with a weak bladder, but a civilian mechanic, whose job it was to ensure that the equipment was in good working order before the day's watch was let loose on it.

Those of us that had been transferred from the obsolete CH radar to the underground system landed an agreeable day out in June at RAF Stanmore, the group headquarters and main operations centre, as part of our induction. We travelled by train from Martin Mill, learned very little that we didn't already know, and arrived back at Charing Cross with a surprise four hours to do exactly as we pleased. Derek's home at Catford was not a massive distance from Charing Cross, so the pair of us shot off there for a meal and had a bit of time to spare before Derek's father drove us back to the station in his Austin Seven.

At the end of June came a most significant happening on completion of our first six months. This was promotion to Leading Aircraftsman, which enabled us to sew the two-bladed propeller flash on to the arms of our uniforms. This would be evidence to everyone that we were not complete rookies, or 'sprogs', which is correct Air Force terminology. Most important of all, the new rank carried a huge pay increase to seven bob a day, or 49 bob a week (a massive £2.45 in new money). Now that we were enjoying such affluence, we were encouraged to open savings accounts with the post office. I am sure that if I search the darkest corners of my home, I will unearth a book stamped 'RAF Savings', along with my blood transfusion certificate from West Kirby. Surprisingly we were able to save, and I managed to build up a reserve, which was to come in handy when I needed to bring my running footwear up to date later in the year.

At around this time the Commanding Officer, Squadron Leader Inkson, was making strenuous attempts to enforce the camp ruling relating to walking on the grass areas around the buildings. This was strongly discouraged, as the C.O. did not want to see unofficial footpaths across his lovely grass areas. One day, with approximately two minutes to get from billet to mess before the deadline for meal serving, I overbalanced, came off the path, and ran about six paces on the grass. Unfortunately, immediately behind me was LAC Magee, the only Military Policeman on the camp without any stripes. Desperate to remedy his lowly situation, Magee promptly booked me and set up a situation that was pure farce.

The following morning I reported to the orderly room to be tried. With a Military policeman on either side, on the command 'accused and escort left turn', followed by 'accused and escort quick march', the three of us marched out of the orderly room and next door into the CO's office. After 'accused and escort halt', in front of the CO's desk, Squadron Leader Inkson, deadly serious, proceeded to read the charge against me. After asking if I had anything to say in my defence, which I hadn't, I was duly convicted and issued with a reprimand. This was then entered in my records as having been 'admonished'. On return to the billet, the conversation takes the following pattern. The billet members say 'How did you get on ?' to which I say 'I got astonished'.

As it happens, I actually found the CO. to be quite an agreeable person. He had to give the OK for any of my athletic trips, which involved me being off the station overnight, and chatted to me about my progress on more than one occasion. He even seemed interested!

We were now into July. The weather as I remember it was reasonable and the cliff-top paths above St. Margaret's Bay provided good scenic running and walking conditions. It was possible to walk into Dover by this route, a distance of around four miles, which I did occasionally on my own at weekends. One evening during the week, however, Derek and I decided to walk into Dover, have a couple of drinks, and catch the bus back. At a point somewhere in the region of the rear of the castle, we took a wrong path and arrived at a dead end. Just as we were about to reluctantly retrace our steps, we spotted an entrance to what appeared to be a tunnel. It was small but just large enough to walk through.

I don't know where we imagined that we would end up, but since the tunnel led directly in at right angles to the coastline, it should have been fairly obvious to us, that if we were able to get through, we would be inside the castle grounds. This is exactly what happened, although I seem to recall us being surprised at the time. Our next problem was what to do next. The Army occupied the castle at the time, so it's fairly true to say that we should not have been in there. We chanced our luck and carried on, eventually walking unchallenged past the guards and out, very relieved, into Castle Hill Road, from which point the pace quickened quite considerably into town.

I was spending a great deal of time on my own at weekends and spent a fair amount of time doing nothing in particular in Dover and occasionally Folkestone. The cinema should have been a good source for using up time, but I only recall one visit, which was to see Eartha Kitt in *New Faces* Not a classic film by any means, but I had pictures of Eartha Kitt and Ruby Murray on the inside of my locker, courtesy of a pre-services mate, Trevor Skinner, whose father worked in a record shop. Ruby Murray was very popular at the time. Maybe the current generation haven't a clue who she is, but at least her name has been immortalised among users of Cockney rhyming slang, (of which I am one occasionally!) with reference to their favourite Friday evening take-away.

Occasionally, on my return to St. Margaret's from these solitary expeditions, to delay my arrival back in an empty billet, I would spend some time in the Quality Inn, a café opposite The Hope pub. Often I would be the only customer, and I would waste a fair amount of time over a single cup of tea. In my fairly depressed state during these weekends, a few minutes conversation with the not unattractive young lady behind the counter was viewed as a bonus.

My time in the Dover area was only eleven years after the end of wartime hostilities, and we had all lived through this period, even if we were only eight or nine years old at the end. It seems strange, looking back, that wartime events did not seem to occupy much of our thinking and conversation. The area had been the scene of almost daily bombing activity, much of a very severe nature, and was justifiably nicknamed 'Hellfire Corner'. The evidence of Dover's suffering was still there to be seen in 1956. Today, a lot older and hopefully wiser, I am well aware of the degree of bomb damage in the town and the extent of the civilian casualties, but I cannot begin to imagine how the people of Dover managed to lead anything like a normal life on a day-to-day basis. The network of caves in the area, coupled with basements of the larger shops, were converted into shelters, undoubtedly keeping the number of casualties down, but it was still a high figure for any town to bear. I can only remember the names of four Dover Athletic Club members during my very short membership of the club, but two of those four surnames appear in the list of civilian casualties.

The Swingate site, with its array of seven aerials reaching up to 350feet, was visible from the French coast in its exposed position up on the cliff top near to the castle. Like most of the Chain Home stations around the south-east coast it came in for its fair share of bombing raids, particularly during the Battle of Britain in 1940. Generally the radar towers survived the onslaught, but there was considerable damage to buildings and casualties among RAF and WAAF personnel.

One person with a story to tell could have been SAC. John Saddleton. John, a Dover resident, was yet another member of the sizeable Kent contingent at St. Margaret's. We were later to become two thirds of a three-man watch, with Sheff (John Shefford) at Truleigh Hill, but I do not recall the conversation on watch ever running along those lines. I was aware that his father was a prominent police officer in Dover, but I have only recently discovered that he was in fact acting Chief Constable throughout the war period.

From the very start of my National Service, unlike most of my colleagues who valued their regular trips home, I was hoping at some stage for an overseas posting. Hong Kong, Singapore, Cyprus, Malta, even Germany, in fact anywhere that had an RAF presence would have been OK by me. One distinct possibility was opening up during the second half of 1956, not for a permanent posting, but for a short visit, which would have been quite acceptable.

The radar operators at St. Margaret's were being sent, a few at a time, for a two-week training course in Malta, but being new to the CEW system my name was well down the list. All I had to do, however, was stay at St.Margaret's and I would rise to the top eventually.

At the end of July I had been in contact with George Cooper, the boys' club leader at Welwyn Garden City, to make arrangements to take a week's leave and join the club group for their annual camp at Exmouth, where I had spent the previous two summer holidays. The rest were travelling down in the club's ancient coach, but as there seemed little point in me going to Welwyn first, I travelled by train from Dover and had an enjoyable week.

In previous years, we had become well acquainted with the very cheap and very potent local Devon cider, but did not generally treat it with the respect that it warranted, consuming far too much, far too quickly, with inevitable consequences. The campsite was on the cliff edge, two miles from the town centre, and the last bus back was earlier than we wished to return. A two-mile walk back, along the coast road and cliff-top, just about cleared the heads enough for us to take part in the occasional organised midnight swim, or paddle as in my case, being a non-swimmer.

Before going on leave, there had been a certain amount of apprehension among the radar staff at St. Margaret's at the prospect of an unwelcome posting to the Suez area. The situation in that part of the world had been boiling up for some time, coming to a head in July when the United States withdrew their funding for the construction of the Aswan Dam. Nasser nationalised the Suez Canal to provide the necessary finance, thereby leading to British involvement. I returned from my pleasant interlude in service life at Exmouth to find quite a few faces missing at St. Margaret's. Some were from my billet and a certain amount of re-arrangement was going on. What followed is generally well documented, but I felt relieved to have escaped being an active part of that particular episode in British history. Much as I would have liked an overseas involvement, I have to be honest and say that I didn't fancy this one at all.

The billet re-arranging meant that Derek Henry and I were on the move again. This time we moved back across to the other side of the camp, in the area that we occupied during the time of our radar course. This time just three of us shared a five-bed room, the other occupant being Peter Kerwood, an outwardly appearing hard case from the Elephant and Castle area of South London, but generally easy going and harmless in reality.

Life got back to normal. Radar duties, running training, and fairly regular demob parties. These were not held in The Hope, as one might expect, being the nearest pub to the camp, but at The Green Man, down on the beach. This not only involved a walk of around a mile each way, but a descent of 200 or so steps through a wooded and not too well lit area down to the beach. Getting back up again on legs that would have had difficulty on the flat, all added to the entertainment value of the evening. Tradition decreed that the person being demobbed provided the funds for a barrel to be set up on a help-yourself basis, and when that was empty it was a case of buy your own. Since the wages for a National Serviceman for the last six months of service was a staggering three pounds sixteen shillings (£3.80), this arrangement was considered affordable. During this period I was suffering from something that threatened to seriously hamper my enjoyment of these occasions, as after about three pints I began to suffer severe pains in my stomach. Generally it resulted in me being sick, when astonishingly the pains vanished and I was able to rejoin the party. This was a relief, as it was beginning to affect my credibility as a serious demob party participant. These days, I never get as far as three pints, so I am unlikely to find out if the problem has resurfaced.

Although it coincided with an awkward period in my family life, I viewed St. Margaret's as a pleasant posting. It is an attractive corner of Kent, and the camp and the village seemed to blend well. I have no doubt that the camp was good for the economy of the village.

The RAF provided a degree of local employment and seemed keen to foster good relations between the service and civilian communities. The village residents were very much in evidence at the regular film evenings in the NAAFI. One particularly striking young lady who graced these evenings was often to be seen walking her Alsatian dog in the village. Her usual dress of Donegal Tweed trousers and fairly well filled sweater earned her the nickname among my group of 'tits and trousers'. This I can assure you was a compliment. Most of us would have been keen to assist in the bonding process where she was concerned. Unfortunately we knew our limitations. On an availability level, she probably ranked somewhere alongside Pilot Officer Hopkins!

It seemed as if we had been in the Air Force for years. So much had happened that it was difficult to believe that we hadn't yet completed eight months. If I thought that things were settling into a steady routine for me at St. Margaret's, however, then I had another think coming, as someone in an office somewhere decided that the cards marked 'Taylor R.F.' were due for a re-shuffle.

Those of us that had been part of the discontinued CH. radar system were still considered to be inexperienced at the new system. We had not undergone any intensive training to be PPI operators, as we had done for CH. To make up for this we were attending classes run by a member of the St. Margaret's staff, Sergeant Jack Ryles, to not only improve our skills for normal day-to-day operations, but to prepare us for examinations to upgrade (or otherwise) to Senior Aircraftsman, which were due in four months' time. This meant an extra blade on the propeller flash on your arm and a sizeable increase in the amount to be collected at each Thursday's pay parade.

One morning, the comparative peace at one of these sessions was shattered by a Tannoy announcement summoning LAC. Taylor to the Orderly Room. My first thoughts were that Flight Lieutenant Jim Chadwin, over at Sandwich, required the pleasure of my company for an athletics fixture against Maidstone or Thanet or such, so off I trotted with thoughts of an afternoon off in mind. On entering the Orderly Room these thoughts underwent instant modification, as not only was I not required at Sandwich, I was not required at St. Margaret's any more either. The trip to Malta evaporated in front of me.

Spread across the Station Warrant Officers desk were papers posting me to RAF.Barkway in Hertfordshire, to join a course to learn yet a third type of radar, plus a rail warrant to Royston, the nearest station. Within three hours, I was on the train. At least someone in Hertfordshire wanted me!

5. Barkway

My rapidly fading memories of Barkway are of an attractive small village, way up in the top eastern corner of Hertfordshire, no more than three miles from the borders of both Essex and Cambridgeshire. With a population of five or six hundred, it occupies approximately a quarter of a mile of the relatively quiet B1368 plus a few side streets. The presence of a stone milepost showing the distance from Cambridge gives an indication of busier past times. There are stone mileposts in various parts of the country, but the one at Barkway is a bit special. This one is the final one in a set of 16 from Cambridge and has been in the village since 1728. The set is believed to be the oldest surviving set in the country. My recollections of particular buildings are vague, to say the least, and it is probably a sad reflection on our order of priorities that I can nevertheless recall a pub at either end of the village and one in the middle. At the top of the village, a minor road heads off towards the A10, and it was just past this junction that the Air Force camp was situated. I say 'was', but recent investigations lead me to believe that the camp is still there, but currently leased to the United States Air Force.

On a Monday morning in August 1956, I left the train, setting foot in Royston for the first time, despite the fact that my journey from Welwyn Garden City had been a mere twenty-five miles. In the high street I met a beefy Scot called Renwick, who was on an identical mission and together we caught something resembling a bus for the five-mile trip to Barkway.

As the others began to arrive, it became clear that the course had been arranged to retrain redundant CH operators on to a radar system called GEE, which was a navigational aid rather than a plotting system like the CH and the Centrimetric Early Warning systems. A mini reunion was beginning to take shape as John Shefford, Harry Harris, Les Willmore and Trevor Fox, from the original St. Margaret's course, arrived. In all there were fifteen of us on the course including Ernie Bradford from Leicester; Jim

McWilliam from Preston; Ian Roy from Esher; Neville Nicholson from Carlisle and Brian Crocker from Paignton. The latter was the only member of the course with any prior knowledge of the system, having been transferred on to it at his station at West Prawle in Devon.

The instructor, Sergeant Jim Edmunson from RAF Truleigh Hill in Sussex, was pleased to have Brian Crocker as a course member, using him on several occasions as back up to his own knowledge of the system. He was a decent guy who managed to administer the course in a fairly relaxed manner, and as a rugby player seemed to equally enjoy our very regular recreation periods, which usually ended up with five-a-side football.

At least once a week, however, it had been decided that a physical training session would be beneficial to us, and for this purpose a PTI was sent over from the much larger camp at nearby Bassingbourn. It was almost like being back at square bashing. This particular PTI was full of himself and enjoyed being in charge. On some of our sessions he had us kitted out in the normal PT gear, but with boots instead of the regulation black plimsolls. We thought that we had left this sort of attitude behind months ago.

These sessions usually involved a three-quarter-mile run on the road to a large open grass area, where we did a series of exercises, followed by a run back. On one of these sessions the PTI, in his plimsolls, challenged us, in our boots, to a race back to camp, setting off at a gallop ahead of us. A few of us took the bait, but I felt that I had the best chance to deflate him a bit, and the others were looking to me to do the business. I wasn't used to running in boots, but as a regular runner I was considerably fitter than the PTI might have expected. Fuelled by the collective dislike of fifteen blokes, I gradually pulled him back, catching him at about half way. It had been a major effort to catch him, and I am not sure if I could have maintained the pace, in boots, for the rest of the distance. I was quite pleased when he abandoned the race at that point, and we all walked back the rest of the way.

We probably learned just about enough radar theory on the course to give us a rough idea of what was in store. Sergeant Jim was well short of Chief-Tech Youll on the technical front, which may in the long run have been a plus point. Radar was, I found, a subject that could be learned much more quickly in actual operation. The two previous radar systems passed fairly quickly through my memory bank. I recall absolutely nothing about the CH system that I operated for just a few weeks and only slightly more of the underground radar which is referred to these days as the Rotor System. Eventually I did manage to retain a bit more detail relating to the GEE system, probably because I was destined to be operating it for the remaining fifteen months of my service. It will seem more appropriate to commit my sparse recollections of GEE to print when I begin to describe the operation at my next posting, which turned out to be my final one.

All of this of course is totally secondary in importance to what each camp and the surrounding locality had to offer in the way of evening entertainment. The average national-serviceman had fairly simple needs. A couple of decent pubs and somewhere to see an occasional film kept most reasonably happy. Some occasional female company was also fairly well up the list of priorities. Barkway measured up OK on the first two points. Early exploration of the village had revealed the three pubs mentioned earlier. The first and nearest to the camp was a bit bare, but provided a good game of darts, whilst the second was so much to our liking that we never did make it down to the end of the village to check out the third one. The names of all three escape me completely. A serious lapse indeed.

Drinking in the pub halfway along the main street was like being welcomed into the lounge of the landlord's private house, which I suppose it could have been. There were several comfortable armchairs and a settee packed into a very cosy little lounge bar, plus the main attraction, a television. Young people today, in fact probably most people below sixty, have never had to endure life without television. In 1956 there were plenty of us that had grown up without it. Television certainly was a rarity in public houses, so it was quite a surprise to find such an agreeable homely and entertaining atmosphere 'out in the sticks' as it were.

As an alternative, the NAAFI at Barkway was exceptional for such a small camp. It had a full-time manager, a middle-aged single civilian called Ted, who lived on the camp. He was probably in his thirties, but even that seems middle-aged to a nineteen-year-old. The NAAFI comprised two rooms, a comfortable bar with darts and bar billiards, and a television room. This had seats laid out in rows, cinema fashion, and the effect was further enhanced by the large screen on to which the picture was projected. All very advanced for the 1950s. Only the quality of the beer stopped us from spending more evenings in the NAAFI. It didn't compare too well with our home from home down in the village.

The evening groups were usually fairly consistent in their make-up and always included Jim McWilliam, who was without doubt the best comedian that I encountered during my two years service. Jim came from Preston, which has an accent all of its own. When I made my earlier attempt to bring all of this together, I described Jim as a comedian in the Ted Lune style, who actually was from the same part of the country. In 1967 when I made this observation, it was possible that most would understand the comparison that I was making. Now, I am afraid, you have to be of pensionable age for the name of Ted Lune to be lurking around in the darkest corners of your memory.

Jim had a fantastic repertoire of jokes and disgustingly unsavoury songs, all delivered without the slightest suspicion of a smile while the rest of us were falling about helplessly. As willing pupils we quickly learned the words to the songs, which we sang loudly on our way back to camp. Fortunately, most of the route back was uninhabited.

Royston was the nearest larger centre of civilisation, approximately five miles away, with a population of around 6,000. Cambridge was only 16 miles away, but not a realistic proposition by public transport for an evening trip. Just getting into Royston by bus was an education in itself. On the few weekends during the course, most went home, and a double-decker bus of doubtful age provided sufficient accommodation for all who wished to make the journey at the weekend. In the week however it was a different story, as a coach-type single-decker was considered adequate. As the village came before the camp on the route to Royston, all seats and some standing room were taken by the time the bus reached the camp gate. About ten of us would squeeze on, and at later stops the driver would get out and forcibly shove the last person on before struggling to slide the door shut behind them.

We only made this excursion once, when it was unanimously decided that *The Man With the Golden Arm* starring Frank Sinatra and Kim Novak, at the Royston cinema, was an occasion not to be missed. The cinema operated a non-smoking policy, which was very rare indeed in the 1950s. The return bus was timed to coincide with the end of the film. As it appeared that the entire bus-load was in the cinema, the return journey was equally eventful. I believe the bus only operated on a couple of weekdays, which would explain in part the large numbers heading for Royston, particularly if a good film was showing at the cinema.

Sheff (John Shefford) and I were beginning to team up, as we had been together previously at St. Margaret's, and our trips home at the weekend saw us both thumbing lifts on theA1, after somehow having negotiated the five miles into Royston. I was keen to get down to Welwyn Garden City to get in a couple of races for the athletic club, as I had no idea where my next posting would be or how difficult it would be to get to races.

Until Welwyn Athletic Club was formed in1953, there had not been an athletic club in the town since before the war. This doesn't mean that there were no athletes in the Garden City, quite the reverse in fact. A group of enthusiasts in the town all belonged to St. Albans City Athletic Club, and together they were the inspiration for the setting up of the Welwyn club. Most of this group transferred to Welwyn, but not immediately, so the club was launched with a membership consisting of a number of what is known in the athletics world as 'second claim' seniors, plus some enthusiastic juniors. Since the 'second claim' seniors were unable to hold office, I, at the tender age of seventeen, was elected as cross-country captain. I then found myself in the very peculiar situation of having to contact established senior runners to check their availability for races.

Two incredible characters, who were part of the group, 'Digger' Hills and 'Mott' Salmon, were also helpers at the boys' club and were a massive inspiration in my early running days. Digger was a major local star and had recorded some pretty good track times, particularly at one mile. But Mott's main sport at that time was boxing, at which he was a feared local opponent, and he had the physique to go with it. They were good friends, and surprisingly changed roles as well as continuing with their original sports. Digger became a useful boxer, whilst Mott became a determined and keen runner. A large amount of my early running was done from the boys' club, with these two and some other members.

Together with the other local athletes, Harry Wilson, Eddie Kean, Chris Brunning, John Davies, Arthur Taylor, John Hogg, Graham Lindgren, Conrad Spall and a few others, they formed the basis of what became a successful club in a very short space of time. Hardworking officials Bill Mobsby and George Clarke plus a useful collection of local junior athletes completed the line-up. Harry and Chris had good coaching skills, and Harry in fact went on to become a highly respected national coach, with several Olympic athletes, including Steve Ovett, in his care. Chris was my coach, and he served me well in this respect, but in reality he was much more than just a coach, as I've mentioned earlier.

I wanted to continue to be a part of the progress that the Welwyn club was making, and was hoping that my posting from Barkway would enable this to happen. Some of the GEE radar stations that were on the list to receive members of our course were in some extremely remote parts of the country, but one or two were within reasonable reach, so I lived in hope. I managed to make ten appearances for the club on each of the two years that I was in the forces, but at this stage of the story I wasn't to know that I would not be returning to Hertfordshire. The chain of events that was to lead to this happening was not due to start for another three and a half months.

Before posting decisions could be made, there was a course to complete, and the highlight was still to come. This took place a couple of weeks before the end of the course, when I became airborne for the second time in eight months. All of us went by coach to the nearby airfield at RAF Bassingbourne, where we were taken up four at a time in an RAF Anson. This time there was a purpose to the flight as we were shown how the radar was made use of in the aircraft, in relation to what was happening on the ground. We were all issued with 'sick bags', the pilot doing his best to make us use them, fortunately without success

Surprisingly, we actually emerged from this session with a reasonable idea of what it was all about. Coupled with what we had managed to take in from the course lessons, it made us feel almost confident that we would cope when we finally got to our permanent postings, wherever they might be.

We had examined the list of possibilities, some of which did not look too appealing. Although we did not know was who was going where, we did know that we were going to be allowed to state a preference. Previous experience when stating a trade preference had led us to believe that this could be a total waste of time. The possibility of spending the rest of our time at Sennen Cove, a mere three miles from Lands End, was not firing the imagination, neither was Trerew, near Newquay, another Cornish posting. The only person who fancied West Prawle, near Kingswear in Devon, was Brian Crocker. He was already stationed there anyway, and it was close to his home at Paignton. Similarly, Folly, near Haverfordwest on the far side of Wales, Clee Hill, near Ludlow in Shropshire, and Worth Matravers in Dorset were only going to receive votes if anyone on the course happened to live nearby. Nearly 50 years on, this looks quite an attractive list to choose from, but the needs of a teenager are vastly different to those of a senior citizen.

Stennigot, near Louth, close to the Lincolnshire coast, looked a good bet for Harry Harris from Lincoln, while anywhere was probably a long way from Carlisle for Neville Nicholson. My priorities had more to do with how close the nearest athletic club was rather than anything relating to home. Gibbet Hill, near Hindhead in Surrey, looked a possibility, but the one that was getting me the most excited was Truleigh Hill at Shoreham in Sussex, just six miles from Brighton. My life so far, all nineteen years of it, had been more or less equally divided between Sussex and Hertfordshire, and I had actually first seen the light of day at Buckingham Road Maternity Hospital in Brighton, despite the fact that my parents lived around twenty miles or so away, near

Horsham. I don't think that they were on a day trip! It was probably more connected to my mother's poor health, and the fact that she was thirty-nine at the time of my birth.

Going back to where I had relatives was appealing, but so too was the close proximity of Brighton Athletic Club, which I knew to be a strong all-round club with a very good squad of middle and long distance runners. The eagerly awaited posting results duly appeared on the station notice board, and against my name were the words Sennen Cove. Most of the others had not received the posting that they had requested, so there had seemed little point in asking us to state a preference. After some discussion we surprisingly decided upon protest action, converging en-bloc upon the agreeable Sergeant Edmunson, who reluctantly agreed to see the Barkway Commanding Officer, who it seemed had decided the postings.

The second list was far more acceptable with Sheff and I being allocated to Truleigh Hill. Harry Harris and Brian Crocker both got their 'home' postings to Stennigot and West Prawle respectively. I am not sure what requests Trevor Fox and Ernie Bradford made, but Trevor ended up in Cornwall, at Trerew, over 300 miles from his Barnsley home. Ernie, from Leicester, fared marginally better with West Prawle, at the far end of the southernmost point of Devon, somewhere between Dartmouth and Plymouth.

The course finished on Friday 14th September 1956, with the issue of weekend passes and instructions to report to our new stations on the following Monday morning. I was looking forward to the weekend. I had kept up a reasonable level of training at Barkway, on the football field and around the local lanes, much the same as at St. Margaret's. I even did some training with a boxer on the camp, who had been given use of a room, which he had kitted out with a punch-bag, weights, and other boxing items. I politely declined his request for a sparring partner even though he promised not to hit me!

As the Welwyn club was continuing to make good progress, they were beginning to get involved in some better quality events. On the Saturday following the completion of the radar course they were making an adventurous trip across the Thames, to compete in

Surrey Athletic Club's cross country relay in Richmond Park. I had been to Welwyn Garden City the previous two weekends, although not necessarily to home, and had finished third in a trial race to select the team. At Richmond we did particularly well finishing 8th out of 32 teams. Our near neighbours St. Albans, one of the top teams in the South, won the event, but in a year or so we were due to give them a couple of surprises.

Following the weekend break, I was due to meet Sheff at 7.30am at Victoria Station on the Monday morning. Not wanting to risk being late, I decided to travel the short distance up to London on the Sunday evening and to stay overnight at the Union Jack Club, close to Waterloo Station. I have always been pleased that I made this decision, as it provided one of those pleasant memories that stay in the mind forever. The Union Jack Club is a marvellous institution, where any member of the services can obtain affordable accommodation and food while on leave or in transit. I have only made this one overnight stop, but I have used their services on a couple of other occasions. I do not know what changes may have taken place since 1956, but I do know that it is still functioning.

For the princely sum of three and six (seventeen and a half pence) I had a bed in a dormitory and a decent breakfast. For another couple of bob I could have had a room to myself, but after sharing a room with anything up to twenty others for the last nine months, I wasn't fussy. There were about a dozen in this room, and the only drawback was the amount of coming and going at all hours throughout the night. In any event, I was due out of bed at 6am myself. After being gently woken by an elderly steward, I was washed, breakfasted, and under the clock at Victoria Station by 7.30 as arranged.

6.   Truleigh Hill

The number 21 Southdown bus from Shoreham Station dropped us off at the stop in the Upper Shoreham Road, facing directly down Stoney Lane, which led to the domestic site of RAF Truleigh Hill. This would be a most dangerous place to alight from a bus nowadays, as it is right in the middle of one of the busiest roundabouts in Sussex.

A former airman, on a nostalgia trip, would find this area of Shoreham rather different from how he remembered it in the 1950s. The peaceful rural setting of market gardens and well-spaced houses to the north of the Upper Shoreham Road has given way to the roundabout and the slip road to the Brighton by-pass. Behind that sits the Holmbush Centre, home to the large stores of Tesco and Marks and Spencer, with McDonalds appropriately sandwiched in between. Further back, behind the stores, the traffic on the Brighton by-pass roars to and from the Southwick Hill tunnel, a four-lane highway that runs for nearly half a mile below the attractive National Trust land that forms the approach to the South Downs. To the side sits another superstore, Homebase, plus Wadurs Swimming Pool.

Wandering down Stoney Lane, a former airman would find absolutely no trace of the camp among the blocks of council flats that now occupy the site, neither would he find any reference to RAF Truleigh Hill in the libraries of either Shoreham or Southwick. Believe me, I have spent several hours looking. It is as though the place never existed.

But exist it certainly did. Its two newest inmates were favourably impressed as they went through the now familiar ritual of checking in, drawing bedding and finding their allocated billet. The camp, built just four years earlier in 1952, had accommodation consisting of a mere seven billets, some housing thirteen bodies and some nine, for a total population of around 90 when full. A guardroom, a small office block, a transport department, a stores building, a sick bay, a cookhouse, a NAAFI, and an education room completed the buildings on this small camp tucked among the houses on the eastern edge of Shoreham.. All of these were mostly situated around one straight road that ran through the middle of the camp. Three of the billets were along a path that ran at right angles to the road and were separated by a wire fence from Buci Crescent, which ran parallel to the billets. Outside of the fence and on the other side of Buci Crescent was a row of six single-storey semi-detached married quarters. Sheff and I were both on our sixth camp in less than nine months, but this was it, the end of the line. We were to be here for the rest of the duration, and a most agreeable posting it turned out to be.

We were allocated beds in the central room of billet 19B, which was the first of the three billets on the Buci Crescent side. The billet numbering seemed a bit odd for a camp with only seven billets, giving rise to speculation at the possibility of more billets on the site at some time. This is unlikely, however, since the total RAF occupation of this corner of Shoreham was a mere six years.

There was a small individual room in addition to the three main rooms, initially occupied by Corporal Roger Jones from Barry in South Wales, but later by Corporal 'Doc' Kinsey from Leicester. Doc was a good deal older than the rest of us, probably forty-something, and had seen wartime service. Following a break in service he had re-entered at a lower rank. Despite the age difference, he mixed in well and was a prominent member of the cricket team.

Two others shared our room in the centre of the billet, one of these initially being another corporal, Barry 'Rusty' Freer, from Exmouth, the very mention of which stirred up happy boys' club holiday memories of sandy beaches, potent cider and girls from Bristol. Rusty was due for demob, as indeed were several of the GEE operators, so we became senior radar men very quickly. As the old hands departed, in came the new, and a week after our arrival came John Glover from Leeds, and John 'Geordie' Patterson from, as one would imagine, somewhere on Tyneside.

Returning to the first day, as we had made an early arrival at the camp, all of the settling in rituals had been completed early, allowing us a full evening to find out what Shoreham had to offer.

Arrival in the High Street revealed five pubs within about three hundred yards, with two more close at hand in side streets. Just round the corner was the Ritz Cinema. So far, so good.

We chose The Marlipins, an old pub next door to an even older museum building of the same name. At that time the pub was a good old-style village-type local, with a game of shove-halfpenny in progress in one corner, but it has undergone a few makeovers since. That first-day drink was the only time during our service in Shoreham that we were to visit The Marlipins. It was to be fourteen years before I had my second drink there, so I don't think that the brewery were counting on me for survival.

The next day it was down to business. We learned that the domestic site was nowhere near Truleigh Hill. This was the name of the location of the actual radar site where our 'work' action was to take place, a beautiful spot 700feet up on the South Downs. There had been a wartime Chain Home Low radar operation from 1940 on Truleigh Hill. This was decommissioned in 1946 and finally removed altogether when the huge underground complex was built in 1951-52. The GEE system that I was to work on had operated continuously since 1942 in the same buildings. The radar site was about three and a half miles from the Stoney Lane camp as the crow flies, but over five miles as the RAF truck flies. If this appears a peculiar thing to say, anyone who has travelled behind maniacal MT Driver Corporal Ken Paxton on the mostly downhill return run, will know exactly what I mean.

On the up journey, the truck followed what was then the main A27 road past Buckingham Park, before turning inland up Mill Hill. The road continued ahead for a couple of miles, then turned at right angles along the crest of the hill, and the present route of the South Downs Way, the long-distance footpath between Winchester and Eastbourne. For the last quarter of a mile, past what is now the Youth Hostel, the route ceased to be a made-up road, rising sharply uphill on a wide unmade stony track, which the truck negotiated without any apparent loss of speed. The occupants were usually three or four Radar Operators, three or four Radar Mechanics, a Military Policeman plus any others with a need to be on site.

The underground site followed much the same layout as at St. Margaret's, with the Guardroom and aerials enclosed within a wire fenced compound. The GEE operation comprised four large Nissen huts, all completely above ground and enclosed by thick blast walls, which housed the equipment. These were two Transmission Blocks and two Receiver Blocks, equally spaced around the outside of the circular perimeter fence of the underground site. As operators, we manned the Receiver Blocks, whilst the mechanics maintained the equipment in the Transmission Blocks, and ensured that we continued to transmit our pulse at the required frequency.

Although the general layout at the underground site was similar to that at St. Margaret's, the radar system at Truleigh Hill was slightly different and was known as CHEL (Chain Home Extra Low). The construction had involved massive excavation and earth-moving operations but the system had ground to a halt in the month before my arrival in Shoreham after only four years or so of operation. The equipment was kept in place for some time, and a policeman was permanently on duty in the Guardroom there during our period of service. Although our blocks boasted an oven, so that the night watch could cook an evening meal, we had no running water or toilet facilities. We therefore had to collect our water periodically from the guardroom, in a large metal container about three feet high and a foot in diameter. The amount of water collected was usually in direct proportion to the size of the body collecting it, so I usually managed to avoid this chore.

The toilet situation was more of a problem. Since we were a fair distance from any other buildings, the more routine calls of nature were answered by a stroll of twenty or thirty yards out into the field outside the block. Anything more serious involved a 200-yard trek to the guardroom, where a bell summoned the policeman out to unlock the gates. After locking it behind you, he would then have to go through the procedure again to let you out. This was OK on a nice summer day, but not much fun at 2am in a howling gale in January, if the need arose.

At the time Sheff and I were introduced to the GEE system, three watches were in operation. Each watch worked a night duty from 6pm to 8am, followed by the next day and night off. The watch then did a day duty from 8am to 6pm, with that night and the following day off. There were probably adjustments to the system to cover weekend passes and longer periods of leave, and the combined GEE staff of operators and mechanics probably numbered 35 at the most. Even allowing for cooks, policemen, admin, medical staff and drivers, the camp appeared to be slightly under-populated. In the days of the CHEL or Rotor operation, the operatives on this system filled the camp, with the GEE personnel billeted out with local families.

Throughout the war period, radar staff had also been billeted out in Shoreham. Between the end of the war and 1952, however, GEE personnel were billeted at RAF Poling, near Arundel, one of a number of original Chain Home stations that remained in operation until the mid-1950s.

The watch system that I have described operated in the early stages, and apart from occasional weekend passes, it was not providing any other two-day breaks from duty. Later on, we were given the chance to work out our own system, eventually coming up with a brilliant arrangement that involved a 14-hour night duty and a 5-hour half-day either side, followed by a spell of two and a half days off.

The GEE operation was administered from a small site office, close to one of the Receiver Blocks, by three NCOs. Warrant Officer Bill Austin was the boss, ably assisted by Sergeant Peter 'Pop' Foster, who as a mechanic provided the technical input. In keeping with the general attitude at the camp, these two kept a fairly relaxed form of control. They were well liked and their trust was not abused. This was something new; you were not supposed to like NCOs. The third member of the team, Corporal Gene Cardozo, was a bit more formal in his position as Training Officer. Since everyone arrived from training courses with little or no operational experience, it was his job to integrate new arrivals into the system. In the early days he gave me a hard time, constantly maintaining that I was too nervous to become a good operator.

At this stage it is going to be necessary for me to come up with a bit of technical detail, in order to explain the system that we were operating, something that I've managed to avoid up to now. I am often looked upon as a bit of an 'anorak' in some fields, and I can quote extensive athletics, football and cricket statistics from many years ago, although I have problems remembering what happened last year! I also have a very weird ability to come up with the capital city of at least three quarters of the countries in the world, a totally useless asset for anything other than crossword puzzles. A radar anorak however, I am not. Still, there are a lot of them about, and there is a vast amount of information available, particularly on the Internet, for anyone who has the time and inclination .For me, it might as well be in a foreign language, and I have to say that it is not a subject that excites me greatly.

One person in particular has done enormous research, specifically on Truleigh Hill, and although I haven't actually pinched any of his work, I have used it to refresh my memory, and will give him the correct acknowledgement in due course. My own lack of ability to understand much of the theory involved, coupled with the passage of time, will probably mean that there will be some inaccuracies in what I am about to say. It should be enough for a general picture, but as I've said before, I am trying to produce a personal story rather than a technical manual.

Briefly, the GEE network was split into regional areas, with each having a master station, two slave stations, and a monitoring station. The master and slave stations each generated a pulse at a given frequency, with the monitor station ensuring that the others stay 'in phase', which was the term in use at the time. This provided a navigational aid to aircrews who were able, from equipment in the aeroplane, to take a 'fix' from the combined pulses. Truleigh Hill was one of the slave stations in the Southern Area Chain, West Prawle, near Kingsbridge in Devon, being the other. The master station was Bulbarrow, and the monitor was Worth Matravers, both in Dorset.

The Radar Operator, sitting at the set in his Receiver Block, would see his station's pulse relayed on to a television type cathode ray tube, in the form of a 'blip' extending above an otherwise regular line. If the blip vanished, it meant a break in transmission.

Alternatively, it was possible for the pulse to drift away from the designated frequency.

In the former instance, it was the responsibility of the mechanics in the Transmission Block to re-establish the pulse, while the operator had a nervous moment waiting for it to re-appear on his screen. Once this happened, he then had to restore it to the correct reading within two minutes from the time that the pulse had vanished. Failure was considered a serious matter and resulted in the instigation of something called a Daily Operations Report. There were some tense moments waiting for the pulse to re-appear, and as the time drew closer to the two-minute deadline, the operator's time in which to make the necessary adjustments was reduced. .

If the pulse strayed from the correct reading, it was a simple matter for the operator to correct by turning one of two control knobs close to the screen either clockwise or anti-clockwise. The operator wore a headset and was connected to the monitor at Worth Matravers, whose operator was quick to spot any lapse in concentration, with the instruction 'come neg Truleigh', or 'come pos Truleigh', which I hope is self explanatory. In the middle of the night, it was often very difficult to stay awake, and it was not unknown for an operator to doze off and fail to respond to the instructions from the monitor. It was then necessary for the NCO at the monitor station to use the telephone line to re-establish contact. This sparked off an elaborate charade of checking for supposedly faulty headsets, all of which could be heard by the NCO at Worth over the phone line.

By Friday of the first week I felt that it was about time that I had a run. I had run on Sunday at Welwyn, but had not yet run at Shoreham, with the problems of settling in. I was very keen to get over to Brighton to join the Athletic Club, but as I was well aware that they had a very strong cross-country team I wanted to be sure that I had several good training runs behind me before going. I set out from the camp and headed off in the general direction of Brighton. A couple of miles later, going through Portslade, I encountered another runner training on a local park which bordered the road. He ran alongside and told me that he ran for a small local club, Southdown A.C. that served the Shoreham and Southwick area. His name was Ken Richardson, and I did some running with him in later years. I probably should have joined his club. They would have needed me more than Brighton, but I was set on the idea of being part of a larger outfit.

I pressed on, and the road signs started to show Hove, and continued to show Hove for a very long time indeed. I passed the old Brighton and Hove Albion football ground, where I was later to see many momentous matches, including a draw against Manchester United in a League Cup match. It was in this match that a seventeen-year-old kid called Beckham came on as a substitute for his first team debut. Not many are aware that the Goldstone Ground was where it all began, but it was some time before he appeared in a league match. Back on the run, I eventually reached the Brighton border at what I now know is Dyke Road. I then turned and ran back for a total distance of around ten miles, possibly my longest run to date.

That weekend I discovered another athlete on the camp, John Sapwell of Surrey Athletic Club. He was about two years older, having come into the RAF about two months before me, after a spell at Durham University. Following trade training at Worth Matravers, he had come directly to Truleigh around March or April, as opposed to the roundabout route that Sheff and I had taken. Eventually he became part of a group with Sheff, John Glover and myself, plus two others who haven't yet come into the story, which remained in contact after the service days were over. Five of the six of us are still in contact to this day, having regrettably only mislaid John Glover somewhere on our journey through life. John Sapwell was primarily a race walker and had represented the RAF on several occasions in road race events, but he had also done a fair bit of running and was in good shape .The following Monday we ran together for the first time, on what I describe in my training diary of the time as a 'fast five miles'.

Possibly because of his spell at university, we joked about him being the aristocrat of the party, a feeling confirmed one day when he appeared in a maroon college blazer and cravat. Nicknames were very quick to be issued in the forces, and he immediately became

'The Baron'. This has stuck, and he is often referred to as John Baron when the rest of us are discussing each other. I was always known by my pre-service nickname of 'Tich', and it wouldn't surprise me if the others still use it.

The following Saturday I paid my first proper visit to Brighton for nineteen and a half years, the only previous occasion being in 1937, when I entered the world at the old Buckingham Road Maternity Hospital. A rather nondescript block of flats now stands on the celebrated foundations. The purpose of my visit was to witness the finish of the 52-mile London to Brighton road running race. Usually the race was contested mainly by specialist long-distance runners, supplemented by a few adventurous novices at the event, and the field most years numbered around fifty.

Two years earlier, at the boys' club, I had been aware that Digger Hills and Mott Salmon had been putting in rather more miles than usual, and strangely were being joined on these runs by my eldest step-brother, Alan. It transpired that they had entered the London to Brighton race as a team for St. Albans City Athletic Club, and to their credit all finished the course, a massive achievement in particular by the converted boxer Mott Salmon. The 1956 event was not a memorable one, although I do remember being impressed by the sprint finish, after fifty-two miles, of 62-year-old Ernie Simmonds of Thames Valley Harriers.

As it happened, I was in the process of running fifty-four miles myself, but this was over a period of twelve days, as my preparation for my first training session with Brighton Athletic Club. I caught the bus over to Moulsecoomb, where the club met on Wednesday evenings in the Winter season, at a community centre and football pitch, a site now occupied by the Watts Building of the University of Brighton. The programme was much the same each week, a warm up on the football pitch followed by a group run to the outer reaches of the Coldean estate and back.

On my first visit, practically all of the names that I recognised from *Athletics Weekly* reports were there, including Hugh Foord, who was ranked among the top half dozen in the country and Paul Abrahams, a top quality mile runner. We set off at what seemed to me to be a comfortable pace, actually stopping at the halfway point at the back of Coldean to re-group. Immediately the last runner regained contact, the leaders set off again at a furious pace, which continued to the end at virtually racing speed. I was taken a bit by surprise but managed to hold on and give a reasonable account of myself.

One thing emerged clearly from this session. The Dunlop plimsolls had to go. The Brighton guys were all sporting brown leather Adidas trainers, with the trademark three stripes. It looked as though Adidas had spread the gospel along the South Coast, but were going to take a bit longer to reach darkest Hertfordshire. One of the Brighton committee members, Jack Nicks, owned a sports shop in Duke Street called Wisdens, so I went to see him at the weekend and parted company with the enormous sum of thirty bob (£1.50), over half a week's wages, but that was just the start of my problems.

Nowadays, you can buy a pair of running shoes in the morning and race in them in the afternoon. In 1956, you had to put them on and go for a run, and then see how many toes were missing some skin afterwards. You then taped up the toes and went for another run, after which it was possible that different toes needed taping. After initially thinking that I really looked the business in my new shoes, I had to leave them off for a week until my toes healed up. Eventually they settled down, and I was able to look OK amongst my new club-mates.

Towards the end of October I had my first race at Brighton. Although not all of their top men were running, I ran the third fastest time out of nineteen in a handicap race and was pleased to run faster than the local top junior Dave McQuade. The following week I was 12th out of 42 in a match with Horsham, Guildford and Worthing. The fact that four clubs from reasonable sized towns could only raise 42 runners between them was a fair indication of the numbers taking part at the time. There were however very few slow runners, as nearly everyone was of a decent standard. In 1956 joggers hadn't been invented.

Although I was keen to maintain a decent level of training, my running had to be fitted around the radar duties, and getting used to night duty was also a factor to be considered. Generally we settled into a steady routine, with Sheff and I usually on the same watch. For a while the third member was John Saddleton, who had been moved from St.Margaret's a couple of months before our arrival, and consequently was the most experienced member of the team. John 'Sad', as he was usually known, was an ardent Young Conservative, while the two of us although having no real political leanings both came from backgrounds far removed from the standard perception of a Tory household. When the discussions on watch inevitably became political, we instantly became the opposition. Sheff would then astonish me by producing totally invented statistics with a completely straight face, which had poor John Sad struggling.

There were elements about both the day and night watches that were bizarre and unorthodox in the extreme. The day watch had to effect a changeover from one block to another at 12 midday, which not only involved transferring the signal between the two receiver blocks, but also the carting of a miscellaneous hotchpotch of items between blocks for the oncoming night watch to use. One of the three operators went over to the other block in advance, and it was his responsibility to set up the equipment in readiness for the changeover, re-setting the pulse at the correct reading when it reappeared at any point on his screen. His contribution to the equipment transfer was usually to struggle over with the water container.

At 12 o'clock, when operating commenced in the other block, the remaining two closed down the set in the original block, before following a carefully planned strategy for transferring the rest of the equipment. The items in question were one armchair, one broom, one radio, two rubber insulation mats, three plates, one frying pan, one kettle, two log books and any usable food left over from the previous night's watch. The larger of the two carried the chair on his head, while the other one loaded the rubber mats on top, and looped the broom through the arms of the chair. Operator number three loaded himself up with the rest of the gear and the pair then commenced their strange daily 400 yard trek across the field, high up on the South Downs, and in all kinds of weather. It is doubtful if the RAF would use a photograph of this pantomime in their recruiting literature.

The night watch was no less peculiar. I find it difficult to believe that sleeping would be officially allowed at anytime during a night duty. We nevertheless followed what seemed to be a long-standing procedure, boarding the truck with holdalls containing blankets and pillows without challenge. As the whole operation seemed to function with minimum input from either officers or NCOs, it seemed as if discipline in this area was a bit lax. Up to midnight everyone stayed awake, the other two sharing the watch duty on a special arrangement that I had carefully negotiated. My sole duty before midnight was to cook the evening meal for the three of us. The usual food allocation was potatoes, sausages, eggs or corned beef, bread, margarine, tea and sugar. The Air-Force corned-beef bill must have been massive. Whether in the cookhouse or on night duty the stuff used to appear at very short intervals, eventually putting me off it for life. In the cookhouse, the appetising object in batter that you hoped was a tasty piece of fish, often turned out to be the dreaded corned-beef fritter.

Up on Truleigh Hill, we had a 'Baby Belling' cooker in each block and one electric kettle, but no running water, hot or cold. Potato washing and peeling and all washing up had to be done in a minimum amount of water from our metal container, usually cold. How I came to be the cook is a mystery, since prior to the forces I had never cooked anything in my life. Cooking may perhaps be an extravagant description of what took place, since everything went into the frying-pan .I have to say, however, that I was able to produce a mean fry-up, a skill that I have preserved to this day, but unfortunately I have been able to add very little else to my cooking repertoire.

After midnight we drew lots for the watch spells. The first shift, or 'first bind', from midnight to 2.30 got it over with and allowed a five-hour sleep spell afterwards. The 'middle bind' was considered the short straw, since it was difficult to stay awake on the set after a possible couple of hours sleep. The last watch from 5am to 7.30 am had similar difficulties, but occasionally the guy on the middle one felt generous, and carried on through both spells. From 7.30am to

8am everyone mucked in to get the block reasonably cleared up for the day watch.

In the early days the sleeping arrangements fell into two alternatives. One option was a notice board laid across the seats of two wooden armed armchairs, with four rubber insulation mats on top. The other option was an open metal cupboard tipped over on its back, with about six months of accumulated newspapers inside. This wasn't bad, but a bit like getting into a coffin, a feeling that was enhanced when one of the other jokers shut the door on you.

Later on we graduated to blow-up airbeds. Mine was kept under my bed in the billet and served me well for a month or two, until I woke up one morning to hear a mouse having his breakfast on it. We flushed him out, and threw boots at him for a minute of two, but I think that he lived to fight another day, or to chew another airbed. I repaired the airbed with a puncture outfit, but it was never the same again. It went down gradually after about half an hour. If I hadn't gone to sleep by that time, I had to get out and blow it up again. Either way, I always woke up on the hard floor.

In the off-duty periods, things were still at an exploratory stage, and initially we spent our evenings in the NAAFI, which was considerably smaller than the one we had experienced at Barkway, and a lot less organised. It was staffed by one of the airman on a rota basis, and while acceptable for television, food was not available, and the beer was generally undrinkable. However, only a couple of hundred yards or so up the road was the popular Royal George pub, which provided a much better drinking atmosphere, until we discovered what 'swinging' Brighton had to offer. Evenings then stepped up another gear completely.

Meanwhile, we were happy to settle for the delights of Shoreham, and that included the Ritz cinema, which showed some good films, even if they were a bit late arriving at this remote outpost. We saw *The Glenn Miller Story* and *Rock Around the Clock* the latter being very big news in 1956. In some areas of the country, the revolutionary new style of music fired young people up to such a degree that they were unable to resist the urge to dance in the aisles, and do serious damage to the cinema furniture afterwards.

Fortunately Shoreham people were of a more reserved nature, and the week's showing of this particular epic passed without incident.

Apart from the Arundel pub across the road from the Ritz, the nearest establishment for an after cinema drink was the King's Head, which was situated on the roundabout at the Western end of the town, and faced directly up the High Street. Both of these pubs no longer exist, and two others in Shoreham, The Hebe and The Kingston have suffered the same fate. The Kingston and The Arundel were probably no great loss, but the other two were good old pubs with a certain amount of character. The King's Head was an old building of some architectural merit, and it seemed an act of sheer vandalism to demolish it, particularly as the site remained empty for thirty years. Only this year has work commenced to redevelop the area that surrounded the pub. The Ritz vanished many years ago, along with the Luxor at Lancing, the Pavilion and the Rothbury at Portslade, the Odeon, the Granada and the Embassy in Hove, and at least ten others in Brighton.

To have the vast amount of entertainment that Brighton had to offer more or less on our doorstep was a massive change from the situation at previous camps, St. Margaret's and Barkway. We were obviously far better off in this respect than most of our colleagues who had ended up in remote parts of the country. Brighton was really buzzing in the fifties. Apart from the cinemas, there was first class variety and drama theatre, two large and popular dance halls, two piers, professional football and cricket, and countless pubs of all types and sizes. This was also the era of the coffee bars, where it was possible to sit for ages with just one cup of frothy coffee in a glass cup and saucer, and listen to juke-box music.

In summertime, with the holiday and day-trip trade, the town was packed. Even in the winter everywhere seemed busy. Despite all that was on offer, our activities were usually centred around the pubs, particularly as demob parties were coming along fairly regularly. We normally headed in a group straight for a large pub called Chatfields at the bottom of West Street, where there was always entertainment of some sort with plenty of music and singing.

An acceptable and almost identical alternative was Harrisons, on the seafront near to The Old Ship Hotel. In between, in The Lanes area, was a cider bar called Applejohns, which frequently came into the equation. Generally the evening was spent mainly in the larger pub, with a trip out to Applejohns for a couple in the middle. After three camping holidays in Devon, I was well acquainted with cider but not with beer both before and after. The effect was usually quite devastating.

Although the group often got split, we usually seemed to come together for the bus ride back, which was normally by the coast-road route. This involved a walk of about half a mile along Kingston Lane to the camp, which together with the bus ride had a generally sobering effect. Although we may have left Brighton considerably worse for wear on most occasions, we had generally got it back together by the time that we entered the camp. Not that it would have mattered much anyway. Truleigh Hill was not like the larger camps with 24-hour manned guardrooms and police and officers all over the place. In fact it's probably true to say that Truleigh Hill was not like any other camp full stop. No officers actually lived on the camp, and any NCOs with authority of any kind were in married quarters just outside the camp fence. There probably aren't too many camps where you can go to breakfast in tracksuit and carpet slippers. In fifteen months I can only remember one parade, which was unlikely to have impressed any passing civilians in Stoney Lane.

Coming back to the walk from the bus stop, Kingston Lane really was a lane in 1956, not the busy link road that it is today. Alongside some fields, where King's Manor School now stands, was a hedge and a ditch, and this is where Stokoe comes into the story.

Distance and alcohol make the exact details of the story a bit vague, and the fact that Sheff and I have two different versions of the story doesn't help. My memory is that on our way back from one trip we found Stokoe, or Brian Stokes from Wimbledon to be precise, on his back in the ditch having become detached from a group just ahead of us. Sheff's version is that Stokoe was with us, and was lagging behind, and when we went back to investigate, he had keeled over and rolled under a parked car. I tried to get Don, who comes into the picture any minute, to confirm either story, but he had a third version. So where are you Stokoe? We need your confirmation. Mind you, whichever version is correct, I wouldn't think that you are likely to remember.

Whilst we are on the subject of Stokoe, it is not possible to think of him without thinking of The Snack Bar at the coast end of East Street in Shoreham. This was its not-too-original official title, but to all airmen at Shoreham it was 'Jessie's'. The cafe was run by an Italian family, comprising Jessie, her brother Albert and their father. In off-duty periods, particularly after a night shift, we tended to drift down to the town and spend a rather large amount of time there. We were always made welcome, despite not spending a great deal of money, and since Jessie was rather better looking than the other two, the place was always known as Jessie's. The jukebox was on the go non-stop and was dominated by male acts such as Bill Haley, Buddy Holly, the Everley Brothers, and a very young Elvis, who had burst upon the scene that year. Brits occasionally got a look in with Tommy Steele, Frankie Vaughan and Lonnie Donnegan, but again there were very few female acts. Johnny Ray topped the charts for seven weeks in 1956 with *Just Walkin' in the Rain* and Elvis equalled that early in 1957 with *All Shook Up*.

What has all this got to do with Stokoe, you may ask? Well, Stokoe spent more time in The Snack Bar than most, so much so that they gave him a job that started before he left the forces and continued afterwards when he didn't go home. A couple of years later his face stared out at me from the front page of the Shoreham Herald, having shared a decent sized pools win with Jessie and the other two members of the family. Stokoe then became a businessman in his own right, buying the newsagents just across the road from the café. I saw him occasionally, but he didn't remain in the area. I've no idea where he is now.

In the meantime new arrivals were changing the make-up of the famous billet 19B. Dave Glyde from Enfield on one side of London, arrived with Tony Stirling from Sydenham on the other side. John Loft from Burnham Market in Norfolk, Ken Davies from Newcastle Emlyn in South West Wales, and Don Allwright from Sidcup, completed the line-up In six months time, Brian Mickels from Manor Park in Essex, was due to arrive from trade training at Worth Matravers to fill a bed in the celebrated centre room.

I bring him into the story at this point because Brian, Don, Sheff, and John 'The Baron' Sapwell are the four that I have kept contact with over all of the intervening years. Initially, for the first few years after demob, this also included John Glover, but at some stage he went to New Zealand and we lost touch with him.

As with the honorary 'title' awarded to John Sapwell, nicknames are decided in a flash, are sometimes slightly unkind, and take years to go away. The Norfolk accent is probably the most countrified of all of the regional accents, so John Loft became 'John Swede', although he may never have been aware of it. On reflection, he was more up to date than the rest of us when it came to keeping up with the fashion trends of the period. Brian, however, was well aware of his nickname 'Mitch', which was taken from the rotund Michelin man in the tyre adverts. Although not noticeably overweight, he might have had a pound or two that he wouldn't have minded losing and consequently took some good-natured ribbing in his stride, much as I've had to over the years with my severe vertical deficiency. I retained my pre-service nickname, while Sheff got away with a bit of name shortening and Don got away with it altogether.

John Swede, I have listed in my earlier notes as 'East Anglia Clove Drop Consuming Champion', and in this respect I may have done him an injustice. Going by the number of tins that arrived regularly from his girlfriend in deepest Norfolk, he was probably All England Champion. It was said that he had to have them sent from home, as nobody in the local sweetshops could understand his accent.

Don was (and still is I suppose!) about two years older than me, having completed his Carpentry and Joinery apprenticeship before call-up. His main recreational activities were cricket and sailing, having acquired his skills in the latter art during his time at Shoreham, as had The Baron. In both respects he had landed a decent posting by coming to Truleigh Hill. We had a reasonable cricket team, and had matches against other local teams, but a real bonus to Don was that the RAF station had a block membership of the Sussex Yacht Club, based on the River Adur in Shoreham. The station even had its own boat, which was kept at the club. This, I was reliably informed by Don at the time, was a fourteen-foot International, which meant nothing to me then or now. I do know, however, that I had a very scary trip on it. With a totally inexperienced crew of Sheff and I taking our orders from Don, we charged up the River towards the footbridge and then hung out over the side to balance the boat as we 'went about', which I understand is the correct term for turning round. It may not have been scary for the others, but I am a non-swimmer!

We were heading towards the end of my first year, when I would be tested to see if I was suitable for promotion to Senior Aircraftsman. We seemed to be coping OK on our forty-nine bob as Leading Aircraftsmen, but another ten bob a week wouldn't go amiss. I was beginning to worry that Corporal Cardozo might stand between me and the extra cash, as his opinion of my abilities differed slightly from mine, but the goalposts moved slightly during one of our night duties and most definitely to my advantage.

It was rare for Cardozo to do an actual watch, let alone a night one, so I was more than a bit surprised when one night I found myself sharing a watch with him and Tony Stirling, who had only arrived from trade training a couple of weeks earlier.

From the start, he complained that he was not feeling too good, and this continued throughout the evening. At around 9.30pm he telephoned Warrant Officer Austin at home, to obtain permission to return to camp on a van that effected a change of policeman at 10 o'clock. Having assured the boss that I was a perfectly capable operator and quite able to man the rest of the watch with only an operator of two weeks experience for company, he duly obtained his permission and vanished into the night. Fortunately nothing unexpected happened, and we got through OK. In due course I became a Senior Aircraftsman without any problems.

At this time, I was stepping up the running training in readiness for the Hertfordshire Cross Country Championship that was due on the first Saturday of the New Year. Having narrowly missed representing the county in the Inter-County event last year, I was keen to try and make sure this time.

I was doing a large amount of road running and had devised a regular course over the old Toll Bridge, which at that time was still the main A27 traffic route with tolls still being collected. In Lancing, I followed the coast road back through Shoreham and Southwick to Portslade before heading up to the upper road to return to camp. This was around ten miles, and the regularity of the run probably contributed to the knee problems that have hampered my progress for many years.

Occasionally I did shorter runs with John 'Geordie' Patterson, who was on the bottom end of the professional football ladder. He was on Doncaster Rovers' books, but during his time at Shoreham played for the third teams of both Portsmouth and Bournemouth. Mostly though his training consisted of a lot of short sprint work in running spikes. I think he was a bit disappointed to be informed that the posh, nicely manicured croquet lawns, at the bottom of Kingston Lane and among the best in the country, was possibly not the best place for his fifty-yard repetitions.

There were two other footballers on the camp, both locals, who played good quality Sussex League football. George 'Mick' Wheeler played in Division One for Old Varndeanians and today still lives less than a mile from the camp, while Medical Orderly 'Dusty' Miller played in Division Two for Goldstone. To the best of my knowledge, the only other regular sportsman on the camp, apart from John 'The Baron', myself and a few cricketers, was top local racing cyclist Ron Beck. Whilst researching this book, I attempted to trace Ron Beck, and phoned his brother by mistake. From him I discovered that Ron ran a business called Rock Around the Clock. It was nothing to do with music however. It was a 24-hour rockery stone delivery service!

Christmas was rapidly approaching, and it seemed that I had little choice other than to volunteer for duty over the Christmas period. I wasn't likely to be expected or welcomed at home, and indeed my last three Christmas dinners had been in the homes of good friends, 'Gez' Watchorn for the first and Tom Ward for the other two. I had no idea at the time what a life-changing decision volunteering for duty was going to turn out to be.

Our forays into Brighton were all-male situations. The thoughts of unattached eighteen or nineteen year olds are never far away from the opposite sex, and considerable time and energy is spent in trying to lose the 'unattached' tag. Away from home and in unfamiliar territory, the quest is far more difficult. So far I had only managed a couple of very 'brief encounters', which were during my time at St. Margaret's. When I say brief, I mean brief. Neither occasion made it as far as the hour mark! In this respect, a person of my stature is at a considerable disadvantage compared to his normal-sized mates. A male, a mere five feet two and a half inches in height, is restricted to a possible field of less than half of the available female population, whereas a male of say five feet ten inches has none of these tiresome restrictions to contend with.

After considerable unsuccessful research in the main part of Shoreham, I found a distinct possibility only a few hundred yards up the road from the camp, behind the counter of the local Co-op. There were three small shops on a parade next to the Royal George pub, a newsagent called Billingtons, a Co-op grocers and a Co-op butcher. Two young ladies were employed in the grocers and both were called Joyce. To avoid confusion, one was re-named Jo, and this was the one that I was targeting with a painfully slow strategy. She fitted my strict height qualification too.

My main tactics were to go to the shop immediately before our night duty at around five thirty, on the pretext of buying fruit or cakes to supplement our perfectly adequate evening meal rations. The truck would then pick me up outside the shop. Just before reaching the shop, I would take off my service beret, comb my hair, of which there was a reasonable amount in those days, and stick my beret under the uniform flap on my shoulder. This, coupled with some suave conversation, I felt gave me a better chance. Anyway, I began to think that I was making some headway, as not only was I always served by the correct person, I seemed to be getting a surprising number of bananas for a shilling!

Just prior to the holiday break came the traditional Christmas dinner in the camp cookhouse. Service custom at these occasions is for the officers to serve the men, but here we had a problem as the total officer strength at RAF Truleigh Hill was just one. Poor old 'Rig', as we called Flight Lieutenant R.I.G. MacDougall, the Commanding Officer, would have been a bit pushed to serve the lot of us on his own, so as far as I can remember, Warrant Officer Bill Austin, Flight Sergeant Perry, and sergeants Jolley and Foster must have been pressed into service to assist.

The chief cook, Corporal Vic King, had a fair amount of flair for the special occasion, and ably assisted by his trusty staff, Snowy Carpenter, Dick Bridges and Bill Burton, he came up with a good meal. The latter was a total 'one-off', and the very mention of his name will bring a smile to the face of any former Truleigh man.

My first service Christmas arrived, and I was due to spend the day itself seven hundred feet up on the South Downs, and apart from a few farmhouses, a fair way from civilisation. Before this was to happen, however, those of us remaining on camp awaited the Christmas Eve dance at Shoreham Town Hall with eager anticipation. Even Shoreham was swinging at Christmas in the fifties.

By the time we made it into the dance, we were fairly festive, having spent at least a couple of hours in nearby pubs, but we were far from being incapable. Immediately we arrived at the doors to the main hall on the upper floor, the band stopped playing and announced the interval, so it was back to the pub for another one, with no indication at all of what was coming next.

Within a few seconds of arriving back in the hall, my pulse rate went up a few notches as I spotted, all on her own up by the stage, Joyce, my generous dispenser of bananas from the Co-op. She wasn't really alone, having come to the dance with her two cousins Shirley and Pauline, who were about three or four years older in time, and about ten in social skills! Full of the confidence that comes with having consumed exactly the right amount of beer, I strolled casually across, and bowled her over with a smooth line of chat. She pointed out her cousins, who were on the dance floor and had been quick to spot what was happening. They were already indulging in a spot of 'nudge, nudge, wink, wink', across the other side of the hall and had an air of 'mission accomplished' about them. I took her home from the dance, but as we arrived at her house, the front door opened and her father whisked her inside before there was a chance for any action. All was not lost though, as I had managed to negotiate our first date on the way home.

A week later, I rolled out the red carpet and took her to see Dean Martin and Jerry Lewis in *Pardners* at the Ritz in Shoreham, after which she said that she didn't want to go out with me again. This was not in the script at all. I was most disappointed as I felt that the evening had been quite successful, but resolved not to give up. In the meantime I consoled myself with a large amount of running, clocking my best ever month's mileage of 146 in January.

I had run in the annual Boxing day race in Brighton, and had finished fifth behind Hugh Foord, Dick Newington, Paul Abrahams and Bruce Theurer, and so felt I was in good shape for the Hertfordshire championship on January 5th. One place behind me that day was John Hay, who I still run with regularly and who is still remarkably fit and competitive at the age of 79! In those days the Boxing Day race started from outside the large Co-op store in London Road, and went to Stanmer Park gates on the A27 and back. We spread out across the London Road to start, and ran out on the left hand side of the Lewes road. On arrival at Stanmer Park we ran round a pointsman standing in the middle of the A27, returning on the other side of the road. For obvious safety reasons the race is now run on mainly traffic free roads around Preston Park. Anyone familiar with the current almost motorway layout in the area close to Stanmer Park would understand that finding a volunteer for pointsman duty today might be a bit difficult.

Before the county championship race, which was traditionally held on the first Saturday in the New Year, there was a little matter of New Year's Eve and where best to celebrate it. As Radar Operators we must have had a pretty good scanning system for finding the best local action, as New Year's Eve saw us adding a new venue to our already extensive list of watering holes.

The Farmers at Lancing, we were advised, was the place to be and so it was. A good evening was crowned at midnight when the lights went out, and two young ladies dressed all in black, but with fluorescent designs on their tops, danced on the bar. Pretty advanced stuff for the 1950s!

To get into the Hertfordshire team I had to finish in the first nine in the county race, but even this didn't guarantee me a place if someone of obviously better qualifications had not been able to run in the championship. As it turned out, this was exactly what happened. I ran the best that I have ever run to finish eighth, only ten seconds behind Dennis Cannon who was sixth, but ended up as first reserve. Derek Wood, from Barnet, the previous year's champion, was selected with the other place being held for Watford's John Merriman, who three years later was to place eighth in the Olympic 10,000metres. I couldn't really have much argument with having to make way for these two, but at least I was first reserve.

The Inter-County race, involving the selected nine runners from all of the English Counties, was in two weeks' time. I continued to train hard, possibly too much so, as I was informed on the Thursday before the race that I was in the team, as Derek Wood had withdrawn. The race was to be held at the British Thompson Houston Works at Rugby in Warwickshire, and I had been sent a train ticket for a specially chartered train from Euston to Rugby.

On the Saturday morning I set off early and on my way to the bus stop met Joyce heading for work. I proudly told her that I was off to run for my county at a big race in Warwickshire. She seemed impressed, and it was only when I was on the bus that I realised that this would have been a good time to push my case for a second date.

The day turned out to be both an experience and a disappointment. The trip up on the train full of athletes was exciting for a young runner such as myself. On arrival at Rugby, as I boarded one of a fleet of coaches which were to take us to the course, the first person that I saw was Doug Penn, who I remembered from my time at Dover. Doug had done well to get a place in a strong Kent team. Top names were everywhere. Warming up before the start, I spotted Olympic stars Ken Norris, Basil Heatley and Derek Ibbotson, plus a host of other major names from the cross-country world. We lined up in pens, nine from each county, with the best at the front. I was eighth in the Hertfordshire pen, with only Dave Woodward from Barnet, who had also been promoted from reserve, behind me. A couple of pens along, I noticed Derek Smith, who was with me at St. Margaret's, in the Gloucestershire team.

The speed at which the pens emptied was frightening. Our top man, Dennis O'Gorman, must have run at least fifty yards before I got out of the pen. For the whole seven and a half miles I felt that I was struggling to maintain a fast enough pace, ending up 259th in a field of 315. Dennis Cannon fared no better finishing 255th, but Dave Woodward, who was behind me in the County race did a little better at 218th. Dennis O'Gorman was brilliant in 7th place, confirming the promise that three years later resulted in a place in the British team for the Rome Olympic marathon. Hugh Foord, Brighton's star runner, was two places behind in 9th place, to lead the Sussex team, but for me the Inter County experience was over at nineteen. For various reasons, I was never to get another chance.

After January's efforts I was feeling a bit jaded, but managed to get it back together for the No.90 Group Championship over a really tough course at RAF Henlow. Barbed wire fences, ploughed field and a river, which had to be waded through four times, was not the ideal course for the shortest and lightest guy in the field. I remember a runner getting hooked up on one of the fences, but nobody considered stopping to offer assistance. Fortunately the group was not strong on cross-country-runners, and I managed third place behind two decent quality club athletes, G.Ewing from Victoria Park A.C. Glasgow, and Norman Roberts from Cambridge Harriers, both representing RAF. Stanbridge.

This race was on February 1st. Later in the year I received a very nice hand written letter, dated 11th September, from Flight Lieutenant 'Monty' Mountfield, the top man in RAF cross-country circles, apologising for the delay in sending me my medal.

In the next couple of weeks I came up with two ways to make my running training more interesting. The first was to run down to the camp after duty at the radar site, which would require assistance from the other two blokes on the watch. It necessitated me getting changed and leaving about fifteen minutes or so before the truck was due to arrive to change the watches, leaving the others to take my uniform back to the billet, an arrangement to which they agreed quite happily.

The radar site on Truleigh Hill sits 700 feet above the domestic site, approximately five miles away. All of the descent, however, comes in the first three and a half miles, before the road levels out for the final section, making a fast and exhilarating run. After about a mile the road makes a sharp ninety-degree turn at Beeding Hill. This sharp turn was known to airmen, but not to locals, as 'Charlie's Corner'. For years I have thought that it was named after a civilian mechanic from Beeding who was collected and dropped off at this point by the RAF transport. I have recently learned that Charlie actually had his own transport. On one misty return trip he approached the corner at great speed and overlooked completely the need to make the sharp ninety-degree turn. Ending up in the field opposite, with considerable damage to fence and car, Charlie, it seems, survived without too many additional problems.

Over the years that have followed, I have run many miles in this area, my current home being a mere three and a half miles from the Radar site guardroom, which is still there and which I can see if walk a couple of streets from the house. Some of the runs today are done in a group from the nearby sports centre, often including this stretch from Beeding Hill to Truleigh Hill. Over the years I have managed to get local people, with no RAF connection at all, to refer to 'Charlie's Corner'. With a bit of luck, it could become part of Sussex legend.

The RAF truck drivers that used to hurtle along these downland roads at incredible speeds were not the only ones to be doing so in 1957. What is already part of local legend is the film *Hell Drivers* starring Patrick McGoohan, Stanley Baker and Herbert Lom which was shot partly on those very roads and in adjacent fields. Perhaps they had lessons from Jack Baldwin and Ken Paxton, the RAF drivers. There is a scene in the film where a truck goes over the edge of a quarry and catches fire. On our way up one morning we spotted the truck roped up on the edge, but when we came down after duty it was gone. It looks as if a good day's filming took place while we were in our Nissen huts nearby.

Returning to possibilities for providing variation to my running training, the second method was to drag some of the other guys out with me. With a great degree of persuasion I managed to get a group together to do three mile runs on a circuit involving Middle Road, Eastern Avenue, the Brighton Road, and Kingston Lane. For The Baron and the footballer 'Geordie' Patterson, the runs were easy. For some of the others that I had roped in, it wasn't such a simple matter. Sheff, who had invested in a new royal blue tracksuit for the purpose, arrived back in the billet practically close to death and collapsed in an exhausted heap on his bed. I then used to make matters worse by taking off my own tracksuit and declaring that I was now off to do my own training, before going off and completing a faster second lap.

In the spring and summer, to be transported up to such a beautiful spot to carry out our duty periods was a privilege rather than a chore, with fantastic scenery in all directions. Two miles to the East was the celebrated Sussex attraction of Devils Dyke, while the views to the West stretched out to Steyning Bowl and Chanctonbury Ring. To the South was the sea, and from the back of the site on a clear day, the North Downs were visible in the distance. I wasn't the only one to be impressed. Kipling was moved enough to write:

> Ditchling Beacon and Chanctonbury Ring
> They have looked down on many a thing
> And what they may have missed between 'em
> I reckon Truleigh Hill has seen 'em
>
> Rudyard Kipling, *The Run of The Downs*

To add to all this, we had sheep. Loads and loads of sheep. The soles of our studded Air Force boots were stained a permanent green from sheep's poo. The sheep were all over the field that housed the radar blocks, and we became used to being on hand to assist in times of difficulty. Occasionally, particularly before shearing, one would get tangled in a barbed wire fence, and we would do our best to free it without getting a severe kicking for our troubles. It was also possible for one of them to lie down and be unable to get up; such was the weight of fleece on its back. We learned how to get behind the sheep and grab two handfuls of fleece and pull upwards until the animal was able to get a grip with two feet. Once this had happened, it was quickly onto four feet and away like a shot.

Best of all was the lambing. With my country roots, I considered that being able to watch lambs being born at such close range was a grand experience. Several times I watched from the doorway of the radar block as a ewe sat down no more than ten yards away, and a few minutes later set about tending to a new family. The lambs stagger to their feet in amazingly quick time, the ewe cleans up, and off they go.

On odd occasions when a ewe rejected a lamb, we have even taken the lamb into the radar block and fed it some warm milk, before phoning the farmer, who would come and place it with a new parent. They didn't teach us any of that on the radar course at Barkway!

Air Force life trundled on, and in fact followed much the same pattern throughout the rest of my service, until close to demob time when yet another radar system was to become obsolete on me. In the meantime, it was duty periods up on the hill, off-duty-periods down in the town at Shoreham, and a fair amount of running training and racing in the evenings and weekends. Social activities changed a bit, as although we were still getting out and about in groups, I had bumped into Joyce a couple of times and had finally ground her down and got her to agree to give me another chance.

For our second date I went a bit more up-market than the Ritz, and took her to see *High Society* at the Granada in Hove, and while she was still reeling from the sheer extravagance, followed it up with a visit to the Essoldo in Brighton. That really won her over, and after that we settled down to seeing each other on a regular basis. After our initial shaky start, I began to feel that I was on to something permanent, and that is what it turned out to be. Forty-nine years and still counting!

From time to time I meet someone from Shoreham who is of a similar age, and if the conversation gets round to the RAF, their main memory is of the parties on the camp that locals were invited to. I can only remember one of these in my time, and yes, it was memorable. The main dining part of the cookhouse was transformed into an agreeable party venue, plenty of music and booze laid on, and an absolutely magnificent array of food prepared under the directorship of boss-cook Vic King.

There was obviously a great deal of talent in Vic, waiting to be released from the mundane daily routine of corned beef fritters and chips, and the array of party food prepared for the occasion was of the highest standard. Whether he learned these skills through RAF training or outside of the force, I have no idea, but he didn't seem to get many opportunities to use them.

Vic King and his wife were one of six couples that lived in the married quarters facing our billets from the other side of Buci Crescent. Flight-Sergeant Perry was the highest ranked of those actually living at the camp, followed by Sergeant Jolley, the Station Warrant Officer, which is probably the service equivalent of Office Manager. Corporals Cardozo and Baldwin have already come into the story, and the final one was occupied by LAC Ken Morris from Tooting and his wife, who were awaiting the arrival of their first addition to the family.

The Commanding Officer lived off camp in one of the smart roads immediately to the West of Buckingham Park. He strolled into work each morning in civilian clothing, complete with brolly and briefcase, only becoming an airman once he had changed into uniform in his office. He wasn't a bad old boy, and the relaxed atmosphere of the camp in general probably radiated down from the top. Don would have appreciated having him as CO. more than most, as it was likely that the arrangement with the Yacht Club stemmed from the CO's interest in sailing.

Next to him in rank was Warrant Officer Bill Austin, who also lived off camp in Downside, at the top end of the park. He was our boss on the GEE Radar operation, and he was fair, straightforward and generally friendly. He expected the same qualities back in return, and apart from the sleeping situation on the night duty, he usually got it. I have a suspicion that he was turning a blind eye to this anyway. Recently whilst rummaging amongst the mountain of memorabilia that is stored in our loft I came across our wedding cards. As our wedding was nearly three years after I left the Air Force, I was amazed to find a card from Bill Austin and his wife.

Once we had come down off night duty, we didn't feel the need for sleep, although in the early days one of us occasionally went to bed on Wednesday morning until after the routine billet inspection. This meant that as the curtains could be left drawn the room did not get too close an inspection.

Usually, however, we headed off down into town, and until the better weather arrived when we made for the beach, it was usually into Jessies for a couple of hours. Just occasionally when we got ideas above our station and fancied somewhere more posh for our mid-morning refreshment, we ventured down to the end of the High Street to the splendid old building that was the Queen Anne Tea Rooms. The lovely black timbered and white plastered building is still there. Thankfully, as a listed building, it is unchanged but for the sign which now reads 'The Indian Cottage Tandoori'. I suppose this is the way of progress these days, and I am as partial to a 'ruby' as anyone. I just can't get used to the idea of it being served up in such an essentially Olde English building.

I am now hoping to claim a first in the area of the documentation of Shoreham's recent past. I own a few books on the subject, and have read others, but nowhere have I found reference to The Readwell Library. Why anyone should have needed to pay to borrow books is a mystery, but there it was, opposite The Snack Bar and a mere hundred yards from the town's official library. If, as temporary residents, we could be granted membership of somewhere as exclusive as The Sussex Yacht Club, getting us into the library should have been a piece of cake. But library members we were not. So we paid our fourpences and patronised the Readwell Library on a regular basis. Sheff at the time was ploughing through *The Complete Works of Shakespeare* at an alarming rate in order to keep the cost down, while Don reminded me recently that he registered under the name of Fred Nerk!

From the middle of February to the end of April, I embarked upon a hectic racing schedule involving a considerable amount of travel. I am conscious that the volume of athletics detail in my story will interest a few and bore many, so I will try to keep it brief.

Since I felt that I was in pretty good shape, I was hoping for a good run in the Southern Junior Championship over six miles on the famous Epsom Racecourse. The junior age group covered the ages 18 to 21, but once reaching 18 it was permissible to run in either senior or junior events. In the 1970s Dave Bedford took this to the extreme by winning the Southern senior race over nine miles, and followed up by winning the junior six miles half an hour later.

On arrival at Epsom, I was in for a surprise. Welwyn Athletic Club had entered me for the senior race instead of the junior, so I had my first experience of flogging round three laps of three miles, finishing 136th out of around 500. If I thought it was going to be any less eventful at the National Championship the following month, I was due for another surprise.

The National race was on the notoriously heavy Parliament Hill course on Hampstead Heath, less than three miles from Sheff's home. We arranged to go up to his place and stay Friday and Saturday nights, making travel to the race on Saturday a simple matter. My race prospects took a knock on the Thursday, when during my final training run in the Shoreham Beach area a ferocious dog took a fancy to the meaty part of my leg, just below my bum, sinking his teeth a fair way into it. After running back to camp with some difficulty, I had an injection at nearby Southlands Hospital and waited to see how I felt the following day.

Everything felt OK, so we made the trip, spending an enjoyable Friday evening with Sheff's brother and his Dad in his Dad's typically London local, with plenty of music and singing and dancing. On Saturday, the Parliament Hill course was its usual disgustingly muddy self, and despite having to run with a bandaged leg, I felt fine for the first half of the race. On the second lap however it all went completely wrong. The leg stiffened up and I struggled round the rest of the race losing positions all the way, eventually ending up a disappointing 268th in a field of around 400. Afterwards, comparing myself to others that I knew in the race, I felt that I could have made the first 100.

Worse was to follow. Bearing in mind that the youth age group and the senior runners had already finished their races, I was one thousand, three hundred and sixty first in the queue for the washing facilities. The mud-removal facilities for a big race at Parliament Hill in the 50s and 60s had to be seen to be believed. A large outdoor area was screened off and a huge number of tin baths were topped up at regular intervals from a large boiler. I haven't been to a race there for many years, so I don't know if things have changed. I do know that removing a large amount of mud with luke-warm water that had already served several previous users is an exercise that does not guarantee the best of results. I didn't fancy going back to Sheff's home in this state, so Sheff recommended a visit to the public baths at Camden Town, which was on the way back. By public baths, I mean baths to wash in, as opposed to baths to swim in. These were commonplace in all large towns in an era when many houses did not have the luxury of a bathroom.

Everyone should experience a visit to public baths. It is an education in itself. After paying for either a first or second-class bath, which determines the quality of towel issued, you sit in a waiting room until your turn comes. All of the water controls are outside of the bath cubicle and operated by attendant only. After agreeing that the water temperature is to your satisfaction, the attendant closes the door and you get in. If you then decide it is not quite hot enough, you call out 'Drop of 'ot in number five!' The attendant turns on your hot tap and goes off to respond to a call of 'Drop of cold in number fifteen!', by which time your bath is reaching crisis point and you have to leap out sharpish and shout for the tap to be turned off. It could be the other way round, in which case you don't have to get out, you just have to sit there as the water gets colder and wait for the attendant to get to you. Far from being a one-off experience, this was to be my regular Saturday morning routine at the old Cobden Road baths in Brighton for the whole of my first year after demob, which is another story and will come later.

Back again with athletics, at the end of March it was off to Essex to run for Welwyn in the Chingford Road Relay. In addition to its early members, the club was starting to acquire some quality runners who had moved into the area to work. Joining Harry Wilson, Arthur Taylor and myself in the five-man team were Geoff Goode, formerly of Belgrave Harriers, who had moved up from South London, and Hugh 'Paddy' McEleney, who I assumed had moved from somewhere across the water.

I travelled up to London early, to take advantage of an early morning low fare, and now being aware of the existence of the Union Jack Club, stretched out on a sofa in the lounge for a couple of hours before making my way to Chingford. We finished 11th in a large field only 30secs behind the sixth team, continuing our progress at higher level. We weren't causing St.Albans any trouble yet, as they won the event, four minutes ahead of us.

Somewhere in the midst of all of this running, service life was still continuing. The next development involved a small, square, one-roomed building that we passed several times every day, but had never been inside or for that matter had ever seen it open. This was grandly referred to as the Education Block. Somewhere in the system was an equally underused education officer in need of a challenge so the two were brought together in the form of a GCE O level English Language course.

The final part of my full-time schooling was of a secondary technical nature, and although our coursework reached O level standard, for some reason or other we didn't take any exams. I saw this as a chance to get at least one O level, and in fact managed to persuade the education officer to enter me for the maths exam as well, but without taking a course.

It looked as if the regular NCOs had been issued orders to attend as they all started, along with several National Service volunteers, but none of them finished the course. In the end only the dynamic duo of Shefford and Taylor made it through to the exam, which was due to be held along the coast at RAF Tangmere in May.

At Easter it was back on the train again for the Potters Bar Under 21 Road Relay on Easter Saturday. This was for teams of four, and we felt that we had a good enough team to make a reasonable challenge. Whilst I had been in the forces, an old friend and workmate from the comb factory period, Michael Staines, for some reason, unknown to anyone, nicknamed 'Wilbur', had been making fantastic progress. We also had John Wenk, who in three years time was going to represent Britain at 800 metres in the Rome Olympics. The fourth member was Don Verlander, a very promising runner who was a couple of years younger, but already performing at a high standard. This was a big event, important enough to attract the top junior teams from North and South of the Thames in Southgate Harriers and Hercules A.C., as well as leading clubs such as Belgrave, Blackheath and Enfield among others.

John Wenk took the lead-off leg handing over to me in fourth place, but ahead of both Hercules and Southgate. I gradually passed the other three and approached the finish in the lead without knowing what was going on behind. As it happened fellow RAF runner and top junior Ernie Earl had been making ground on me for Hercules, but I sent Don Verlander off for lap three with a lead of around forty yards. Don held on well, losing out only to Hercules. Wilbur held second place right up to the final fifty yards when Southgate's star man squeezed home by three seconds.

We felt that we had done the club proud. Southgate had been the top junior team in the North London area for some time, and we had held them to just three seconds. Wilbur had the fifth fastest lap of the whole race, I was seventh and John eleventh. At the presentation, I met yet another celebrity, as I received my third team place award from former world mile record holder, the legendary Sydney Wooderson.

Welwyn had their money's worth from me that weekend, as on Easter Monday, I ran the Bognor ten miles road race for them, my first attempt at racing the distance.

Training at the Brighton club had switched from Moulsecoomb to their summer base at the splendid Withdean Stadium. It was originally built as a tennis venue, but was now used almost solely for athletics. A cinder track had been laid only the previous year, and the whole arena was set in a natural bowl with dense trees on two sides. Along the finishing straight was a rarity, a mock Tudor, council-run, public house, The Withdean Sportsman. It all made for a fantastic setting that the London clubs loved. I was pretty impressed myself. In my career to date I had run about sixty track races, but only four on cinders. Now I was not only to get regular racing on cinders, but was going to be able to train on it as well. All of this was a far cry from Handside Lane Playing Fields at Welwyn Garden City. Synthetic all-weather surfaces were still a long way off.

At the time of writing, however, nearly fifty years on, the stadium is the subject of major local controversy. Brighton and Hove Albion Football Club, lost the Goldstone Ground, their home for one hundred years, to retail development. After a period of ground sharing with Gillingham, they moved into Withdean Stadium as a stopgap until a new ground was built. The three athletic clubs that use the stadium have become very much the secondary users, and are continually inconvenienced by the needs of the football club. I find my loyalties slightly split here, for although my priorities lay with my number one sport of athletics, as a supporter of the football club for nearly fifty years I would like to see them resolve their ground problems quickly.

Plans are in place for a new community stadium on an unattractive brown field site at Falmer, between the two Universities, but they are being met with considerable local opposition. For some unfathomable reason the final decision lies with the Deputy Prime Minister, John 'Two-Jags' Prescott. Hopefully, by the time anyone reads this, he will have made it.

Back in 1957, however, I made a good start to the track season with a new best 3 miles time of 15mins 24secs and convinced myself that I was going to be a better three miler than a miler. This was the pattern that I followed in the RAF events that were coming up. Very shortly, in the space of five weeks, I was due to run in four further races at this distance, three of which were RAF events, plus a one-mile event.

Before all this was to happen, the two survivors from the O level English course, having saved the luckless education officer from complete humiliation, now had to face the possibility of being cut down to size by failing the exam. The two of us set off for RAF Tangmere, famous in Air Force folklore for its Battle of Britain and Douglas Bader connections, and slept on mattresses on the gymnasium floor in readiness for an early morning kick-off. We both passed, but I had to go back again later to try and justify the education officer's faith in me, having entered me for the Maths exam without my taking a course. Sadly, I let him down, and after demob had to slog through a year of once-a-week evening classes in order to rectify the matter. It is often said that nobody ever uses the mathematical knowledge gained early in life to assist in later work situations. Oddly enough, I became something of a curiosity in a most of my jobs, as I retained a fair working knowledge of trigonometry. This served me well until the advance in computer programmes took away my genius status, reducing me to the level of my co-workers who probably had far better education but inferior memories.

Now, I am afraid, comes a big lump of athletics. I feel a bit apologetic about inflicting this upon readers, but not too much, as it all culminated in an appearance in the finals of the RAF Championships, which was the biggest thing that happened to me in a relatively ordinary athletics career.

Before I embark on any of this, it is going to be necessary to try and explain the system of qualification through station, group and command championships in order to make it through to the big one. The situation was made complicated by a very strange set-up regarding the chain of command governing the Truleigh Hill station.

The underground radar operation at Truleigh was governed by No.11 Group, which in turn was part of Fighter Command. The GEE radar that I was involved with was however part of No.90 (Signals) Group, which for some strange reason had command status and entered its own team in the championships. I was actually given the opportunity to qualify through both channels and started off on the No.11 Group route first. This was altogether the toughest way, as Fighter Command was far and away the strongest command athletically. Another factor was that on the No.11 Group side, Truleigh Hill came under a parent unit, RAF Wartling, near Bexhill, so I had to get through their camp championship first. This meant a total of three qualifying events

I was wary of the Wartling race as small camps often had two or three good distance runners, as I had found to my cost last year, when I didn't make it into the RAF Sandwich team. Wartling had Mike Tribe from Redhill and Reigate A.C. and Ray Roseman of South London Harriers among their inmates. Tribe was a decent half miler and miler, and Roseman, whose home was in Brighton, and was well known to me, eventually ran a sub four-minute mile. Fortunately they chose the two shorter events, while I ran in and won the 3miles. Wartling does not exist now as an RAF station, but the buildings are still there, having undergone a couple of changes of use, initially to become Her Majesty's Prison Northeye.

John 'The Baron' Sapwell and 'Ginger' Monksfield came over with me from Truleigh, John having no trouble in the 2miles walk, while Ginger finished second to me in the 3miles. The next step was the No.11 Group event at the impressive RAF Stadium at Uxbridge, where Robin Campbell of Essex Beagles won easily in 15minutes exactly. Half a lap behind, with 15mins 40secs in second place, was me, so I had survived the next stage. This was going to be the end on this particular route, however, as also in Fighter Command, but in another group, was the reigning RAF. Champion Colin French.

John and I felt that we now needed to go for the No.90 Group option, which meant only one qualifying stage, the actual No.90 Group Championship. We didn't even have to get through a station qualifier as Truleigh could enter this one direct, and nobody at Truleigh was challenging either of us for a place.

RAF Henlow, the venue for the No.90 Group event, was a large camp with good facilities, although obviously not up to Uxbridge standards. Uxbridge was, after all, the RAF's showpiece as far as sporting facilities were concerned. The grass track at Henlow was in very good shape, and there was a fair bit of ceremony attached to the whole affair, as one would expect from the largest station in the group. I had actually run there two years earlier, in a match for Welwyn against the station team.

Although No.90 Group had command status as just a single group, it was nevertheless quite a sizeable group, with a fair sprinkling of decent club level athletes, and one real super-star on the women's side in Corporal Janet Pearson, the top athlete in the whole of the Women's Air Force. Among the men at the longer track events were Derek Haith (Thames Valley Harriers), the National Junior half-mile champion, Malcolm Edwards (Sheffield) a rising star in his part of the country, and Norman Roberts (Cambridge Harriers) and G.Ewing (Victoria Park Glasgow), who had both beaten me at the Group cross-country. Haith was entered for the half-mile, Edwards, the mile, and Roberts, the steeplechase, leaving me to battle with Ewing for the three miles. Last year's winner Jackson from RAF Chigwell was also in the field.

I had my little moment of glory here, as I took the lead at the 2miles point and went on to win by 12 seconds from Ewing in 15mins 33secs. I was a bit disappointed with the time, but I had booked my place for the 'big one' as did John later in the afternoon in the two miles walk. No. 90 Group did not have too many medal prospects for the RAF championships, and it was unfortunate for John that one of them happened to be a walker. John had to take second place behind Flying Officer Ian Paul (St. Albans), but both of us could now look forward to the big day in two weeks' time at Uxbridge.

If the story is starting to appear as if athletics was taking over from service duties, then for about a month in the middle of 1957, this is how it was. I was now due to report back to Henlow the following Monday, to train there for a week, before going to Uxbridge early the following Monday for the championships, which were spread over three days.

On the Monday at Henlow, we were subjected to a massive circuit training session in the gym, all of the squad doing the same session, irrespective of event. During a breather between parts of the session, I spotted someone heading in my direction, and I was instantly transported back in time nearly ten years to junior school. Coming towards me was a formidable all round sportsman from Welwyn Garden City, Eddie Caswell, who was in the team as a javelin thrower. I had not seen him at the championship and had not even known that he had a talent for the javelin.

Welwyn Garden City in some respects is a strange town. It is split down the middle by the railway line, with the only means of crossing at the very bottom of the town, and close to the top of the town. Most of the private housing is on the west side, with most of the council housing on the east side. Residents of both sectors refer to 'the other side'. While I was at junior school we lived on the west side, moving over later for reasons that are too complicated to explain.

I went to Parkway Junior School whilst most on the 'other side' went to Peartree School. Very rarely did the two groups mix. One occasion when they did was for a cricket match between the two schools. Somehow I found myself in the Parkway team despite being not very good at batting and totally useless at bowling. Possibly there were a lot of withdrawals by those who feared that they would be captured and held hostage. Football was a different matter. I was a dashing eleven-year-old inside-left for the school team, and my hero was Billy Steel, the most expensive footballer in Britain at fourteen thousand pounds.

If you have lost the plot in all of this build-up, we are now getting round to Eddie Caswell. To all of the kids on our side of town he was held in awe as a fearsome opponent at everything. He was the best bowler, best batsman, best footballer, in fact best everything. He was eight feet tall and ate ten Shredded Wheats for breakfast. He had just demolished the wicket of our number ten, and I went in at number eleven, a two-feet-six stick insect, with the truly frightening task of facing the last three balls of his over.

Three times he went back for what seemed an enormous run, and hurtled towards me at amazing speed. Three times I said my prayers and held out my bat in the hope that the ball would either hit it, or the wicket, rather than my little body. Three times the ball either whizzed past or thudded against my bat, sending shock waves everywhere. The over ended, and my team-mate was out during the next one. I was nought not out and very happy to have escaped with that. Three balls from Eddie Caswell were enough for me. Eddie went on to be a major local sportsman and I had seen him from time to time, but I didn't even know that he was in the Air Force, let alone in the same team as me for the championships. He didn't look quite so tall in the gym. We chatted for a while, but

I didn't talk about the cricket match. He would probably have been surprised that I saw it as such a big deal, but believe me, it was.

At Henlow, we trained hard on the track on Tuesday, Wednesday, Thursday and Friday mornings, with a five miler on the road on Friday evening for good measure, before going down to Uxbridge for our mini-Olympics early on the Monday morning. At Uxbridge we were housed in the gym in bunk beds, and the atmosphere was quite special. There were over 500 competitors plus officials, with Fighter Command having the largest squad at over 70. Transport Command had the smallest with just 27 competitors, while we had 52, drawn from 13 different stations. Realistically we didn't have too many medal hopes. We were banking on one first place from Janet Pearson, and Warrant Officer Mann was also a possibility for the Hammer title. Among the others only Derek Haith and Ian Paul looked likely candidates for medals.

Although the events were spread over three days, my event was a straight final, so I was not due for action until the final day. I was able to sit in the stand and watch the rest of the events. There was a sizeable crowd, not only from the large number of athletes awaiting their events, but there seemed to be interest from the general public as well as other airmen in the area.

The standard was high. An advance look at the programme told me that there were twenty runners in my race, six of whom I recognised instantly as being really top-level performers. The mile looked as if it would be a fast race with Peter Clarke, Ian Boyd, John Herring, Ernie Earl, Stan Taylor and Brian Fernee in the field, while the sprints were real class with Dave Segal, Roy Sandstrom and Mike Ruddy.

There was a degree of inequality, which was inevitable in service racing. Those of us that had come into National Service at eighteen, were either still in the junior age group (17-19) or in the first senior year, as in my case. For those who had been deferred to complete an apprenticeship or university course, there was the definite advantage of already having the experience of a couple of years of senior competition. Finally, the regular airmen could be of any age and be quite seasoned campaigners. Quite a few of the athletes on display still had their best achievements ahead of them, but were still nevertheless performing at a high level on their way up.

The final day arrived, with, as one would expect, bags of ceremony, including an Olympic style march past of the teams. Whatever our athletic standard, we all knew how to march, even if some of us hadn't done it for some time. Wednesday 3rd July was one of the hottest days of an already good summer. Not good for twelve lap running. It was very uncomfortable warming up, but it was the same for everyone. The race was due at 15.10hrs, and the talent around me out there in the centre of the arena was making me feel as if I was in the wrong place. In the fifties, top international athletes turned out to help their clubs in quite low-key events, and twice I have had the privilege of lining up alongside Gordon Pirie. But this was something different. This was quality en masse. To indulge myself I have listed the complete line-up (see next page).

Well, this was it. A line up of twenty runners for the biggest race of my life, but I cannot remember very much of it at all. I can bring to mind incidents from many races, many years ago, but this one has almost gone completely. Thankfully, I have always been a diligent record keeper, so I have the bare facts from my training diary of the time. I know that I got carried away with the excitement of the occasion, and started too fast with a first mile in 4mins 49secs, at which point I was probably only about 10secs behind the leaders. I slipped back on the second mile, and struggled badly in the heat on the third, but so did most of the others. I eventually finished 10th in 15mins 33sec, the same time as the 90 Group race, but in far more testing conditions. My records say that I was a bit distressed afterwards, but I was pleased with my placing.

At the front of the field Colin French retained his title in 14mins 10sec, with Alastair Wood second in 14mins 28secs. In cooler conditions French may have hoped for a bit faster, and Wood probably a lot faster. In third place Bill Rigby, with 14mins 42secs, did well to hold off some of the better-known names. My records, written at the time, state that both Reeve and Langridge, obvious medal candidates, dropped out of the race around the two mile point. I hope that I am correct and that I have not done them an injustice. The weather seriously affected the times in the two longer events, the three miles and the steeplechase, but not the mile, which was won by Peter Clark in a speedy 4mins 9secs.

Table 1: List of runners

Fighter Command	
SAC Colin French (Shaftesbury Harriers)	RAF 3 miles Champion 1956 3rd RAF CC 1957
SAC Robin Campbell (Essex Beagles)	2nd National Jnr CC 1958 2nd RAF CC 1957
Technical Training Command	
F/O Alistair Wood (Aberdeen A.C.)	4th European Marathon 1962
AC Roly Langridge (S. London H.)	Surrey Snr 3 miles Chmp 1957
Individual Entries	
P/O Mike Reeve (Polytechnic H.)	Nat. Youth CC Chmp 1954 RAF CC Champion 1957
Cpl. Bill Rigby (Worksop H/Thames V.)	13th RAF CC 1957
Maintenance Command	
LAC Don Taylor (Grimsby/Herne Hill)	British 10k record holder 1963
AC J. Hawes	10th RAF CC 1957
Coastal Command	
Cpl. W. Shearer	7th RAF CC 1957
F/O C Pierce	Not known to me
Bomber Command	
LAC M. Moody	Not known to me
Sgt. M Carnelly	Not known to me
Transport Command	
SAC A. Berry	Not known to me
LAC John Bratt (Oldbury Harriers)	Decent quality club runner
Home Command	
LAC Ray Batty (Thurrock Harriers)	Decent quality club runner
LAC F. Myers	Not known to me
Flying Training Command	
Cpl. H. Palmer	Not Known to me
SAC T. Hurst	Not known to me
No.90 Signals Group	
SAC Roy Taylor (Welwyn A.C.)	Decent quality club runner
SAC G. Ewing (Victoria Park Glasgow)	Decent quality club runner

Finishing 10th in the RAF final sounded good to me, but I wasn't under any illusions. All of the finalists in the mile could have beaten me over three miles. Also, some good athletes were most likely eliminated in the Fighter Command and Tech. Training Command Championships, bearing in mind the quality of their representatives in the three miles final. I definitely would not have made it through the Fighter Command route. Although I may have had an easy passage to the final, I did have the satisfaction of knowing that eight finished behind me, which meant that I had beaten runners from at least four other commands. I certainly felt capable of a better time, and three weeks later I ran 15mins 5secs in the Brighton club championships.

As a team we got our expected winner when Janet Pearson, the 1956 winner and record-holder at 100 and 220 yards, retained both of her titles. Cpl. Brooks added a further medal with third place in the high jump. The WRAF athletes were not restricted to one event as were the men. Warrant Officer Mann missed the hammer title by less than two feet, for our solitary men's medal. Ian Paul had a near miss with fourth place in the walk, and I think that Derek Haith may also have been fourth in the half mile. John's memory is a bit frayed round the edges regarding his position in the walk, but he thinks that he was eighth. I wrote the names of the first seven in my programme, so this seems likely. As it happened, he would have survived the qualification through the Fighter Command route as he beat both of their representatives in the final. In the men's team event, as expected, we were at the back end, placing eighth out of nine, ahead of Coastal Command and very close behind Transport Command.

Being able to escape to athletic competition does not make my National Service experience a typical example. Coupled with the fact that Truleigh Hill was really a dream posting compared to some of the larger, more highly disciplined camps, it is not surprising that I am able to look back on it all with a great degree of affection. A relaxed attitude to discipline, an unusual working situation high on the beautiful South Downs, a beach within easy reach, and all of the various delights of nearby Brighton, was not a situation enjoyed by every National Serviceman. Many who were less fortunate with their postings hated every minute of it.

The next big thing to occur was that I bought a made-to-measure suit. I had been in the forces for over eighteen months, and I was still wearing the same civilian clothing that I had worn for most of the year before call-up. In the Welwyn Garden city of the 1950s, clothes shops were none too plentiful, and anybody who was anybody among the teenage population 'went up to London' to buy their first suit. Kings Cross Station was exactly twenty miles from Welwyn Garden City. In the year before call-up, in search of a suitable tailor to honour with my first suit purchase, I emerged from Kings Cross Station to consider my options.

Across the road, opposite the station, was a gents' clothes shop called Leaders. Within an hour I had bought a fairly light-coloured suit, off the peg, plus a pair of black trousers and was back on the train. Unfortunately, as I do not have an off the peg body, the suit jacket was too long and so were both pairs of trousers. The idea was to wear the light jacket with the black trousers, which was the 1950s equivalent of 'cool'. The jacket being long was OK, and was fashionable at the time, but I had to sort out the trousers. I was unlikely to get any help at home, so I set about shortening the black pair myself, which I managed without actually cutting any material off. Thus for two years I had been wearing these trousers with several layers of material hidden in the last few inches. These were the clothes that I had with me at Truleigh Hill and that I considered were due for a sizeable update.

Later on, back in the year prior to call-up, clothes buying exploration extended a bit further than immediately outside Kings Cross Station, with forays into the previously unexplored territories of Islington High Street and Chapel Street Market.

In the final six months of Air Force service we had the huge weekly sum of three pounds sixteen shillings at our disposal. This was a devious recruitment attempt to make us feel so well off that we would all rush to sign on for a longer period. Although generally unsuccessful, it allowed us to boost our savings accounts, which were already fairly healthy. I had splashed out two pounds seven and six on a posh red pair of Addidas track spikes in May, but

I still had enough in reserve to fund a visit to Burtons for my first made-to-measure suit.

It was a new experience, to have a man poke about between my legs with a tape measure, and ask me intimate questions about where my private parts rested, but I was pleased with the end result. Charcoal Grey was the colour that everyone was wearing, and I felt very smart. I had to remember that I now had a girlfriend, who I needed to impress on a regular basis.

Yes, I know that I haven't mentioned her for quite a few pages, while I've been getting all of this important running stuff out of the way, but she is still in the story, and we've now survived six months. I must have felt that it was starting to look like a permanent arrangement, as I started to think about my future, bearing in mind that I was due to be released out into the big wide world, with no home and no job, in less than six months.

During the early part of my service, I was entertaining the idea of going to Australia, on an assisted package as it was called at the time. You could get there for just ten pounds, on the condition that you stayed for two years. Tradesmen were especially being encouraged, and I suppose that with three years of an apprenticeship completed, I was 60% of a tradesman. Who paid the fare to come back, if you didn't like it after two years, I hadn't got as far as finding out.

By now, however, those thoughts had undergone some serious revision, and I was now looking at the possibility of staying in Sussex. I had completely dismissed the possibility of returning to Hertfordshire, and any vague thoughts of solving the home and work problem, by signing on for a further spell in uniform, had also gone out of the window. If I was going to have to start again from scratch, at the age of nearly twenty-one, it might as well be in Sussex where someone cared about me. Mind you, Joyce and I had to survive another six months together, which we did. I think the suit helped.

I had this vision that Crawley, very similar to Welwyn Garden City as a new town with large factory estates, was the place to start looking for a job. I felt that I had to continue to consider myself as a toolmaker, for the time being at least, and see if I could get a decent firm to take over the remaining two years of my apprenticeship. Getting this bit sorted out seemed to be the main priority. I couldn't do anything about finding somewhere to live until much closer to demob.

It was easier than I expected. The Employment Exchange (the 50s version of The Job Centre) gave me a few possibilities, so I headed off to Manor Royal, the largest factory estate in Crawley, and got fixed up at the first call. I was very relieved to have sorted out that aspect of my future, and thought that it would be a simple matter to get the paperwork transferred from Welwyn Garden City. I went back to camp and celebrated by taking a week's leave with Joyce, during which we had a day overseas at Shanklin, on the Isle of Wight, and another in London. The highlight of the London day was a trip to Battersea Park, where all of the attractions installed for the Festival of Britain celebrations in 1951 were still in place.

The summer of 1957 was exceptionally hot. I have photographs taken during that period that would suggest that my origins were rather closer to the Equator than equally split between inner-city Nottingham and rural Sussex. After night duties, we spent a lot of time on Shoreham Beach. Ken Davies became so tanned that someone once said that he looked like a foreigner, to which we all replied 'He is. He's bloody Welsh'. At that time large sections of Shoreham Beach area were still undeveloped, and our favoured spot was opposite the end of Ferry Road. In daytime off-duty periods, we tended to stick around Shoreham, with a fair bit of time being spent in Jessie's as well as on the beach.

There were also evening trips to Buckingham Park for cricket matches against local teams. I can only remember one of the opponents, which was Ricardo Engineering, their team at the time being called Bridge Works. I have already documented my cricketing deficiencies at some length, but I was nevertheless a very important member of the squad.

I was the scorer. Now I may have been a rubbish cricketer, but I was, and still am, interested in the game, and was in fact an experienced scorer. As a schoolboy, I had often scored for Welwyn Garden City, at their lovely ground at the bottom of Monk's Walk in Sherrardspark Woods. Don was one of the stars of the Truleigh

Hill team, and continued to play regularly in the Worthing area for many years. 'Doc' Kinsey and 'The Baron' were also prominent team members, but here the memory runs out, apart from, you've guessed it, the after-match sessions across the road in the Green Jacket.

I wasn't the only one to be forging close links with the local population. Don too found his future wife, Anne, during his time at Shoreham. John Glover and Mitch tried a different line, and joined the Methodist Youth Club, both with some success, although not permanent. Five marriages resulted from 1957 partnerships that I am aware of. There may have been more, and none of the blokes had far to walk, since all of the girls lived within three streets of the camp. For closeness however it would have been difficult to beat Radar Mechanic Jim Stiff, who was billeted out with a local family in Stoney Lane immediately opposite the camp gates. Jim married his landlady's daughter, Dawn. Apart from a brief spell back home in Grimsby after demob, he has remained in the area ever since.

Pete Mawer was the only one of the five to be married during his service time, but sadly Pete's marriage was the only one that didn't make it into old age. Pete and John Hewitt, from Ilfracombe, married sisters, and although John initially stayed in Shoreham, he took his wife back to Devon after a short while.

In contrast to the first year of service, where I had experience of six different stations, the entire second year was spent at Truleigh Hill, following much the same routine each day. There were very few personnel movements, and consequently a lot of us can look back on quite a lengthy spell in Shoreham. As I've often said, it was a good area to be in, and offered plenty to do.

Ask any person of a certain age what they remember most about Brighton in the fifties, and you can be sure that the Regent Ballroom will come into the conversation somewhere. At the weekends, it really was the place to be. If you look at a Brighton bus today, across the front you will see the name of a person who has made a major contribution to the history of the town. People from all walks of life are included. The name of Syd Dean can be seen on one of these buses, and whenever I see it, I am back in the 50s and 60s.

Syd Dean's band was the resident big band at the Regent for many years, and very good they were too. If they had to take a week or two off for holiday, it wasn't sufficient to call in any old band to replace them. Major names such as Eric Delaney and Ken Mackintosh were signed up to deputise. The place was usually packed, and the sprung floor bounced under the weight of jiving couples. Many couples met for the first time at the Regent, and many got engaged there, including a young former airman and his young lady from the Co-op.

The Aquarium also boasted a sizeable ballroom and staged weekly dances, which in the main were not as spectacular as those at the Regent. But they did have the upper hand on a few occasions in the year, when their dances featured the bands of Ted Heath and Ronnie Scott, the really big names of the day.

I was now dividing my leisure time between Joyce and the group events from the camp, as well as getting in a reasonable amount of running training and track racing. The demob parties and other occasions for celebration were tending to swing away from the big boozy Brighton pubs, and for a while the main venue was the Swiss Cottage in Shoreham. This had been a major entertainment centre in Shoreham way back in the 1800s and early 1900s and had struggled on in a lesser fashion ever since. There was usually some form of musical entertainment, and the boating lake was still in use in the nineteen fifties. The consumption of large amounts of alcohol usually encouraged a fair degree of unruly behaviour on dry land. The presence of the boating lake added a new dimension altogether. There were several instances of participants at our events ending up in the water, and I am sure that they were not the first.

Generally though, I think that we were improving with age. The boozy events were becoming less frequent, though not before Sheff had scarred me for life at one of them. The occasion escapes me, but I can remember that we all arrived back in the billet a bit worse for wear and in a fairly stupid mood.

Sheff grabbed his mug and decided that a visit to the cookhouse for a cup of tea seemed a sensible idea. The rest of us decided to stop him, probably a wise decision at that time of the evening. After a series of drunken rushes for the door had been thwarted and he had been dumped back on his bed, he made a swift exit through the window. We rushed out of the door, bringing him down on the grass outside of the billet. In the resulting scramble he swung his arm round and his mug smacked me straight in the face immediately below my nose. There was a large amount of blood, and I headed for the mirror expecting a massive wound. When the blood had been cleared away, the result was a cut less than a quarter of an inch long, but the scar is still just about visible nearly fifty years on.

In September for a few years in the late 50s and early 60s, Brighton Athletic Club staged a fairly impressive floodlit athletics meeting at Withdean Stadium, which usually attracted a fair number of international stars. There were also a couple of events for the ordinary club athlete, including a mile. I had fancied myself as a three miler all summer, and had only run a couple of mile races. But I felt that my best time was due for some improvement. I managed to get it down to 4mins 36secs, and it was just as well that I ran in this event as it proved to be the end of my season. The following week I caught a dose of Asian Flu, ending up in the sick bay for a few days.

I have never heard of anyone catching Asian flu since that period. I'm not sure that I understood the difference between Asian and everyday flu then or even now, but I certainly do remember how totally drained I felt, and how every movement was difficult and painful. The medical orderly, another 'Dusty' Miller, had a certain amount of training but nothing to enable him to cope with this. A doctor from the town, Dr. Partridge, was called in, and he made the diagnosis and advised the treatment for me and the other two who were in the same boat.

I am not sure whether the presence of the other two helped or retarded recovery as they were two of the major jokers on the camp, and we spent a great deal of time laughing, which in itself was a very painful exercise. They were the two 'Gingers',

Monksfield and Darling. They haven't come into the story other than a brief mention of 'Ginger' Monksfield running the three miles with me at Wartling. 'Ginger' Darling came from Watford, where I had spent my last two years at school, and whilst at Truleigh Hill he became a member of a local amateur dramatic group. Joyce and I went to see him in a play at Lancing, where he performed with some distinction. He also played in goal for a local football team during his time in Shoreham.

The three of us spent three days together in a mixture of pain and comedy. Just getting out of bed to go to the loo was a major operation, and I am surprised that the after-effects did not last longer. In all I only stopped running for two weeks but missed two races that the Welwyn club would have liked me to run in. There was a major road relay at Chelmsford at the end of October, and I needed to get back to fitness for that.

The Chelmsford event proved to be the major breakthrough that the Welwyn team had been threatening for some time. We finished fifth out of fifty-two teams, and received a glowing write-up in *Athletics Weekly,* the athlete's bible. It was clear that we were not yet good enough to beat our local rivals St. Albans, unless they had anything other than their best line-up out, but this is exactly what happened. Our team, however, of Harry Wilson, Geoff Goode, Hugh 'Paddy' McEleney , myself, Michael 'Wilbur' Staines and Arthur Taylor was probably the best that we could raise.

I took over from Paddy in 4th place, with Geoff Allen of St. Albans breathing down my neck, and managed to open the gap to about 200 yards at the take-over point. Although we dropped a place over the final two stages, we managed to maintain the lead over our local rivals St. Albans. We fielded the same team in a cross-country fixture two weeks later and caught them napping again. Possibly of more significance that day was that we also beat a Watford team that included John Merriman, Mike Wiggs and George Howard. This will mean nothing to most, but will register with any elderly athletes that might get to read these memories. In less than five years we had made huge progress to now be capable of mixing it with the big guns, but we were still a comparatively small club.

Radar duties had by now settled into a fairly boring routine, making us doubly thankful for the excellent location from which we operated. Only one third of the time on watch was spent on actual radar operating duties. Even on those spells the demands on an operator were minimal. A minor correction here and there was all that was required, unless of course the pulse vanished altogether. Then all hell was let loose for a couple of minutes until normality was regained.

Inevitably, priorities seemed more directed towards the social scene. As I have indicated earlier, our celebrations for demob or birthdays had swung away from the Brighton pubs, and after a spell at the Swiss Cottage in Shoreham, they took on another complexion altogether. We were now to be found in the agreeable surroundings of Langford's Restaurant in Western Road, Brighton, in our best suits, substituting a three-course meal plus wine for the usual several pints of beer. We had become gentlemen.

Langfords, unfortunately, is no more. The space that it previously occupied is now fresh air, several feet above the bus stops outside of the Churchill Square shopping development. Long before Churchill Square was planned, the shops in Western Road at that point were in line with the rest of the road. To make way for the shopping development, a dozen or more shops were demolished including the large women's clothing store, Dorothy Norman, plus other established Brighton names such as Kendalls, Polyfoto and Macfisheries. Langfords was above one of these shops, and towards the end of 1957 hosted several pleasant evening meals for the newly civilised group of young airmen from Shoreham.

Maybe the influence for the change was initiated by John 'The Baron', who was coming up for demob ahead of the rest of us. Sheff and I had arrived at Truleigh Hill in September of the previous year, and although John had only entered the forces two months ahead of us, he had taken a much more direct route to Truleigh, having been there for some time before we arrived. John was demobbed in November and went back to Shooters Hill to prepare to be 'something in the city' and to get married in due course to Jean.

In keeping with the new image, Sheff, as befits a man capable of reading *The Complete Works of Shakespeare,* reached new heights of sophistication by discovering Drambuie. It was however a short-lived trend, which ended with the expensive agony of spilling almost an entire glass full in the Swiss Cottage one evening.

Just as I thought that things were ticking along nicely towards the end of my service spell, I had a setback when the company at Crawley, where I was hoping to resume my apprenticeship, contacted me to tell me that the deal was off. It looked as if my previous company in Welwyn Garden City had pulled the plug on my plans by giving me what you might call a 'negative reference'. Perhaps I made a mistake here by not going to see them personally. I feel sure that I wrote to advise them of my plans, rather than just leave it to the company at Crawley to contact them. Maybe if I had gone to see them, I could have convinced them that I was no longer the little smart-arse, with plenty of ability but no inclination, but had in two years turned into a responsible, well-adjusted and modest young adult!

Either way, it was back to square one, and my demob date was creeping closer. Early action was needed, so I had to resort to 'Plan B', that a couple of months ago I couldn't see myself using.

Back in the summer, after my maths exam at Tangmere, I decided to thumb a lift back to Shoreham, as it was a straightforward route, totally on the A27. I managed to get a lift fairly quickly with a director of a branch of a large nameplate manufacturing company in the Brighton area, who was returning to his office in Hove.

During conversation, I told him that I was hoping to stay in Sussex and would be looking to try and get my apprenticeship transferred. At that stage, I hadn't been to Crawley. Before dropping me off at the top of Stoney Lane, he gave me his card and said to go and see him if I was stuck for a job when I was demobbed. I hadn't really thought that would be at all likely, and probably neither did he, but as I was now running out of time quick action was called for.

His name was Ted Johnson. I have to say that he was more than a bit surprised when I turned up on the other side of his desk, at a very small factory unit behind Portland Road in Hove. He had completely forgotten the lift back in the summer. There was nothing going at his branch, but to his credit he made an effort on my behalf, by phoning the works director at the main factory in Brighton and arranging an interview for me.

From Ted Johnson, I went straight to the main part of the company, in the Queens Park area of Brighton and was offered a job, to start on Monday 13th January 1958, at seven pounds a week. This was a considerably larger operation, and overall the company employed around 500 people at several locations in the Brighton and Hove area. They were not able to take over my apprenticeship, but I had to make a quick decision and decided to abandon it, as I needed to be earning as soon as possible after demob. Although I had only completed three years of my apprenticeship, I had learned enough to be able to make some of the press tools that they needed to produce their nameplates. I felt that it would do until something better turned up, which it did, sixteen years later!

The next problem was to find somewhere to live. Instead of going off to Crawley to search out a possibility, I had to think about central Brighton instead. For a change luck was on my side. Instead of me finding accommodation, the accommodation found me. My situation was known at Brighton Athletic Club, and fortunately for me, one of the members was looking for a lodger.

Colin Whittingham was a few years older than me, and he was a good quality racing cyclist, as well as a cross-country runner. Colin lived with his mother, within walking distance of the nameplate factory, and they had a room that needed an occupant. The house was in a very long terrace, and was two up two down, and two a bit further down still. The kitchen was on the front in a semi-basement, and it was strange to see feet going past at eye level at the top of the kitchen window. None of the houses had bathrooms, so my 'one-off" experience at the public baths in Camden Town in March, became a Saturday morning ritual at the old Cobden Road baths for all of the next year.

The houses did not have indoor toilets either. The toilets were small brick buildings at the bottom of the garden, built in sets of two, back to back with the one next door. Not everyone can relate the pleasures of sitting on the loo at the bottom of the garden, discussing the issues of the day with the next-door neighbour. Somehow or other you always knew if the person entering next door's loo was male or female. If it was the latter, it didn't really seem quite appropriate to be carrying on a conversation with the lady of the house in such circumstances.

All in all, Colin and his Mum helped me through a year that could have been much more difficult than it was. It was a lively, friendly atmosphere and I felt at home for the first time since my mother's death thirteen years earlier. I paid three pounds five shillings for my keep, which left me with almost exactly the same amount of cash that I had at my disposal during the last six months of service. This however is jumping on a bit. I still had a month to serve before demob, but at least I now knew where I was going when the time arrived.

I had been racing on a regular basis all year, actually totting up thirty-seven races during 1957. An interesting situation arose in December, when my two clubs, Welwyn and Brighton, faced each other in the Bexhill Road Relay. Despite being situated way down in the bottom corner of Sussex, the Bexhill Relay attracted a lot of interest from London and beyond. Welwyn decided to treat it as a Christmas outing, arranging a dinner in the evening in a hotel on the seafront. I ran the fourth leg for Welwyn, my first-claim club. We finished fifth, one place ahead of Brighton. I went to the dinner in the evening, just making it back to Brighton in time for the last train to Shoreham at 1am.

Truleigh Hill was undergoing changes. The radar operation was gradually being wound down, and the camp was thinning out. Bodies were being posted out either to other types of radar or to Gee stations that were still operating. The appropriately named radar fitter, Brian Gee went to Folly near Haverfordwest, a posting that would have suited Ken Davies, who was sent to Ireland instead. Dave Glyde too had an overseas posting to Ventnor on the Isle of Wight, while John Glover and John Patterson ended up at Trerew in Cornwall. The cook Dick Bridges had the longest journey with a posting to Australia.

Sheff spent his last few weeks manning the switchboard, a job later taken over by Mitch. Notes written many years ago, plus information dredged up from my memory, have got me this far in my story, but the final few weeks are a blur. I 'hit the wall', as we say in the running world, when it came to recalling whether I continued on the radar operation to the end of my service or whether I was transferred on to something else. I also could not pinpoint any time when the radar or the camp in general ceased to function.

Mitch came to the rescue. As he was very involved in the final processes, he remembers it well. At least, after a bit of rummaging around in both his memory and his loft, he came up with the goods. He assisted in the dismantling of the equipment at the radar site, and sets this at February 1958, just one month after Sheff and I were demobbed. The camp closed soon after, with Mitch being one of the last to go, even manning the guardroom at some stage. A policing operation continued for a few months, both at Stoney Lane domestic site and the now unused radar site on Truleigh Hill, but Mitch was almost certainly Shoreham's last radar operator. Later research revealed that the GEE system actually ended at Truleigh Hill at the end of November 1957 after 15 years of continuous operation.

Before our demob date at the beginning of January, Sheff and I were planning one last major exercise as our final farewell to the Air Force. All airmen were granted a number of free rail warrants per year, in order to be able to get home on leave, and both of us had one unused warrant left. With less than a month to go, we had to decide what do with the warrants, as to leave them unused was not an option. We looked carefully at how to get the absolute maximum benefit and finally submitted an application to the Station Warrant Officer, Sergeant Jolley, for two return tickets to Wick, the nearest station that we could find to John o' Groats, a round trip of somewhere in the region of fifteen hundred miles.

On receipt of our application, the sergeant became very 'un-Jolley', and immediately applied himself to uncovering the fiddle that he felt sure that we were perpetrating. His suspicions were further fuelled by the presence on camp of Pete Brown from The

Shetland Isles, who he couldn't believe wasn't part of the fiddle. In the end we must have convinced him that we really intended to go, and it seemed that there was nothing in the rules to stop us travelling fifteen hundred miles at the RAF's expense, just for the hell of it.

So on Tuesday 17th December, we set off on what we saw as a three-day trip, but with no planning whatsoever regarding overnight accommodation. We didn't even know where we would be when we would need accommodation, so it was very much a question of sorting it out as we went.

Initially, all went well. We read a bit, chatted a bit, dozed a bit, had something to eat and generally felt that we had pulled a good stroke. The weather was grim, and it was raining steadily. I can't remember exactly where the novelty started to wear off. I would guess that it was somewhere around Preston or Lancaster. We were getting bored and discussing the possibility of cutting the trip short, just as the scenery started to take on an agreeable change as the train proceeded up through Kendal and Penrith, on the eastern edge of the Lake District, new ground already for both of us.

West Kirby had been the northern limit of my travels, and I suspect that it was the same for Sheff. Before the forces, I had been no further north than Nottingham, and Sheff's limit was probably his wartime evacuation to Shropshire, so at the time it must have seemed as if we had achieved something new. If we were going to shorten the trip, the Lake District seemed a good place to do so, and with a major town coming up for the next stop, we made a decision. Looking back now, I consider that our next move was a big mistake. We got off the train at Carlisle and decided to call a halt to our exploration there.

The weather, admittedly, was a deciding factor. When I look at the map and trace the route of the railway line up through the Scottish Highlands, I tend to visualise the scenery as it would be in summer and think that this is what I missed in 1957. However, it was mid December and raining, and there was a long way to go. Even the most inspiring scenery doesn't look quite so good in those circumstances. It must still niggle just a little a bit though; as before writing this section, I found out that a period return from Brighton to Wick would now cost one hundred and twenty six pounds. I could leave Brighton at 6am, and be in Wick by 9.30pm. That doesn't sound bad to me. I wonder if Sheff would be up for it! To this day, despite having travelled extensively in England and Wales, I still haven't been any further north than Glasgow.

Memories of Carlisle are not great. I seem to remember being surprised that people spoke with a Scottish accent. Perhaps I thought that the change came over you suddenly once you were over the border.

We found a bed and breakfast, had something to eat and weighed up the possibilities for a cold wet December night in Carlisle. It boiled down to the usual choice between the pub and the cinema, with James Cagney in *Man of a Thousand Faces* getting the nod as the cheaper and possibly more exciting option.

We were ten miles from Scotland, and we were going to get some stick back at camp for the failure of our grand plan to get to John o' Groats. We should at least have been able to say that we had set foot in Scotland, so after breakfast on the Wednesday morning we boarded a bus in Carlisle for the first place over the border, Gretna Green.

In the fifties, Gretna Green was far more in the news than it is today. Young couples, unable to convince parents that to get married at sixteen or seventeen was the most sensible decision that they were ever likely to make, were arriving at Gretna Green on a regular basis. A thriving business was developing around runaway marriages. It was possible to get married in the blacksmith's shop without any prior booking or other formalities. I do not know if weddings are still performed there, but it is certainly on the map as a tourist attraction today, and it was no different in 1957. We did a quick round of the recognised tourist sites and caught the bus back to Carlisle. It was another twenty-five years before I made my second and only other visit to Scotland.

The general idea now was to head for Keswick and complete a similar comprehensive inspection of the Lake District, staying overnight before catching the train back on Thursday morning. Train to Keswick seemed the best option, as our return tickets covered us as far as Penrith. I remember standing on the curved platform at Penrith and watching a 'through' express leaning over as it hurtled through, and I remember station names of Penruddock and Threlkeld on the single track line to Keswick that no longer exists. I also remember that when we arrived in Keswick in the dark, it was still chucking it down, while we waited in a shop doorway for the pubs to open.

At six o'clock we went in to become the first evening customers in a pub in the centre of Keswick. Fifteen hours later we came out again. Big surprise, it had stopped raining. If fifteen hours seems a long session, I have to say that bed and breakfast was included. Midway through the evening we remembered that we had not made any arrangements for accommodation. Just as we were reluctantly preparing to go back out into the rain to see what we could find, one of us, I'm not sure which, spotted a B & B sign on the wall. We promptly booked ourselves into a double room, with double bed, Morecambe-and-Wise style, and settled down for another couple of hours in the bar.

The talk in the bar among the locals that evening was all about football, just as it was in the barber's shop in my first week at Cardington, and coincidentally for an almost identical situation. The draw had been made for the Third Round of the FA Cup, when the survivors from the lower leagues get the chance to play one of the giants from the top division. And just as it was at Bedford, the local club had drawn a really, really big one. Workington Town, twenty miles away on the coast, who hadn't been a league club for very long, were about to stage the biggest match ever seen in that part of Cumberland. Workington had hit the jackpot and had drawn Manchester United at home.

I have always remembered the conversations in the bar, and the Internet facility has allowed me to look up the outcome, which shows that Dennis Violett scored all of the Manchester goals in a 3-1 United victory, before a crowd of 21,000. These are the bare statistics, but only now, however, have I realised the important connections that make that match part of an extremely sad and historic FA. Cup campaign.

The match was played on the fourth of January 1958, just one month before the Munich Air Disaster that claimed the lives of eight Manchester United players and fourteen others. Five of the eight appeared in the match at Workington. If Manchester United does not always have the sympathy of much of the British football public today, they certainly did early in 1958. Thirteen days after Munich, they had to get together a team to play Sheffield Wednesday in the fifth round. By the time that the programme was printed, they still had no idea who would be playing, and no Manchester United names were included in the programme. Remarkably they made it to the final, losing to Bolton Wanderers on the day. It became probably the most written about campaign in the history of the FA Cup, but outside of Cumbria, it is unlikely that many are aware of the contribution of Workington Town at the beginning.

It is often said that any true football supporter of a certain age will remember where they were when they heard the news of the disaster. I was walking into Pool Valley bus station in Brighton, on my way from my new digs, to catch a bus to Shoreham to meet Joyce, when I saw the news on a poster. On a lighter note, I can also remember where I was when I heard that Roger Bannister had broken the four-minute mile. Mind you, if you've read this far, you may not think that unusual.

But back to the Lake District. On the Thursday morning, we left the pub and walked down to the edge of Derwentwater. We hadn't got a great deal to report from Scotland, but if we were in the Lake District then at least we should have been able to say that we had seen a lake before returning to camp. We must have looked an odd couple, standing there on the edge of the lake in our dark civvy overcoats and carrying holdalls. Come to think of it we probably looked peculiar wandering around Gretna Green the previous morning as well!

Well that was it. The adventure was nearly over. All we had to do now was get back to Shoreham. The journey back by train was fairly uneventful, but we did something that I hadn't done before or since. We had a three-course meal on the train, which, as I remember, started at Runcorn and ended at Watford.

Despite not completing our trip as planned, I felt that we had gone out with a flourish. It had cost us a bob or two for accommodation and food, but had been well worth the effort. All of the travel had been courtesy of the RAF. If we had been getting demobbed in the summer, I am sure that we would have stayed on the train and completed the journey.

It was now the week before Christmas. Very little was due to happen between now and demob on January 8th, as far as the RAF was concerned, but I had a couple of races to complete before then. I was due to run in the Brighton Boxing Day Race, with the Herfordshire championship to follow on the first Saturday of the New Year, the day before I was due to move to RAF Medmenham to be demobbed. I had run well enough to make the county team the previous year and had made good progress through 1957. Getting ready for demob, travelling to Welwyn Garden City and back on the Saturday and then to Medmenham on the Sunday, was not, however, the best set of circumstances to have surrounding a very important race.

I don't remember a Christmas dinner on the camp that year. Perhaps the numbers had dropped so far as to not make it viable. I spent Christmas Day with Joyce and had dinner at her parent's house.

The Boxing Day race went well. I finished third in 31mins 34secs for the six miles, exactly one minute behind star man Hugh Foord, and nineteen seconds behind Bruce Theurer, who was second. It was the closest that I had ever been to Foord over that sort of distance. I was also one minute faster than last year, which looked a good omen for the county race.

Somewhere in that final week at Truleigh Hill, with two of us being demobbed together, it might have been expected that a major demob party would be in the offing. Throughout the last eighteen months, I had been a participant at many memorable occasions, but when it came to my own, it just didn't happen. With the camp running down at an alarming rate, personnel levels dropping, and people being moved to unusual jobs, it is difficult to recall just exactly who was still at Truleigh Hill at the time we made our joint exit. There was a fair bit of billet condensing, and for the last few weeks I found myself in the luxury of a room of my own in a billet next to the cookhouse.

Sheff had been seeing a girl from Southwick during the last few months, and the two of them, plus Joyce and I, went into Brighton for a quiet drink, in total contrast to the noisy, boozy affairs that were commonplace during our early days at Shoreham. Sheff hadn't viewed their relationship as a permanent matter, and so this was the end of the line. I think she was disappointed, but accepted the situation.

The final weekend arrived. I had been to Welwyn Garden City to collect my toolbox, in readiness for starting my new job, but apart from that, everything else that I owned was with me at Shoreham and fitted into one holdall.

All that I had to do now was to go and run for Welwyn in the county race, and get back to camp the same evening. The race was at Welwyn Garden City, but local knowledge of the course was no help. The field was considerably stronger than the previous year, when I made the county team. I wound up eighteenth, ten places down on last year. We were no match for St.Albans when they had a full team out, but we held off a strong Watford team, and I collected my third successive second-team medal. It was a far stronger Hertfordshire team that lined up at the Inter-County event that year. As a relatively minor county with nothing like the numerical strength of the likes of Lancashire, Middlesex, Surrey and Yorkshire, they did magnificently to finish sixth.

I have very little recollection of the couple of days spent at Medmenham, going through the demob process. There were others, including Harry Harris, who had been on both the CH and GEE courses with us. I know that we went into Marlow for the usual evening refreshment, but until recently had very little memory of the area. On my 60th birthday Joyce and I walked the Thames Path from Maidenhead to Marlow, and last year from Marlow to Henley, so I have better appreciation of the area now, than I had in those early days of 1958.

On the final day, January 8th, the Medmenham Commanding Officer made a half-hearted attempt to interest me in signing on for a further spell, before handing me my discharge certificate, which among other things said that I was a cheerful and capable airman. It also said that I was five feet two inches tall. I keep stressing how important that half inch is. I'm small enough as it is, without being further reduced by clerical error!

So that was it; it was all over. Sheff, Harry and I walked down to the crossroads from where we were to catch the bus into Marlow. As it was a cold morning and we had time in hand, we were grateful for the presence of a café by the crossroads in which to waste the time. After a short while, we saw the bus approaching through the steamed-up windows, and left Malcolm Vaughan to sing *Chapel of the Roses* to an empty café. The first part of our final journey in uniform beckoned. For them it was a simple matter to go home and pick up the threads where they left off two years ago. For me, I was heading off into the unknown, to a completely new start. Three months short of my twenty-first birthday, I was starting again, with a blank sheet of paper, on a journey that I hoped would finally lead to a normal life.

7. Conclusions

It must have become apparent long before the last paragraph that my story would have a happy ending. Joyce and I were married in 1960, and we have three daughters and two grandchildren, all of whom I am justifiably proud. Thanks to her, the normal, happy family life that I had hoped for has materialised and continues. I have had excellent dividend from what I discovered in the Co-op late in 1956.

I remained a toolmaker for only one further year, before being moved into the office and staying with the nameplate company for a total of sixteen years. I managed to get through over fifty years of working life and was fortunate not to spend a day out of work. All of my jobs were involved in Production Administration, loosely associated with the Engineering industry, apart from an interesting year managing three hundred young people in the early days of the Youth Training Scheme.

On leaving the Air Force I was quite happy to be forging a new life for myself on the South coast. I was prepared to bring down the curtain on my previous unsatisfactory home life at Welwyn Garden City, despite the fact that my father was still there. From January 1958, when I was demobbed, until August 1959 I cannot recall any contact with the family at all. I did, however, retain contact with the town through Chris Brunning at the athletic club.

It was through this contact that I found myself lining up for a one-mile track race at the newly opened Gosling Stadium at Welwyn that August. My youngest stepbrother, Robert, was at the meeting, and it was with some apprehension that I agreed to his suggestion to go home with him afterwards. This proved to be the start of a bridge-building exercise that has kept me in fairly loose contact ever since. My father was working an evening shift at the local ICI factory and was able to take a short break when I arrived there asking to see him. We had our one and only drink together in the sports club bar. Although he never managed to see me play football or run, at least we had that moment together.

I was 27 when he died from a heart attack at the early age of 52. His first grandchild was born the following year. I received the news of his death by telephone early one afternoon at my desk in the office of the nameplate company. I continued to work for the rest of the afternoon. I wish that it had been different.

A few years ago I discovered that my stepmother's first husband, after remarriage, had created a second family, who were in occasional contact with my stepbrothers. The whole extended family have in recent years staged get-togethers at which I am included, and I am able to attend these quite enjoyable occasions without the bitterness that was generated in the early years.

Memories of my spell of National Service are kept alive by continued contact with four of my former colleagues over a period of almost half a century. I have never been under any illusions about how easy my spell of National Service was and about how others must have had a considerably tougher time, particularly those that became involved in conflict. This has made it easier to recollect and write with enthusiasm about my time in the RAF..

The first to leave the RAF was John 'The Baron' Sapwell, who married Jean and became 'something fairly significant in the City'. I don't think that it was actually in the City, but it makes a good line! He initially returned to his home area at Plumstead but has lived at East Grinstead for many years. He continued to race-walk competitively for a year or so after leaving the service. One of his sons has carried on the running tradition, and our paths cross occasionally at Sussex events. John has played a major part in keeping the five of us in contact by hosting get-togethers at East Grinstead in 1985 and 1994.

Next out, at the same time as me, was John 'Sheff' Shefford, who went back to London to start with, before taking himself off full-time to college in Buckinghamshire, to enhance his business and language qualifications. He is also married to Jean (not the same one!) and lived in Redditch and Portishead before retiring to South Devon. In 1983 and 1984, I had a lengthy spell working in Cheltenham, and stayed overnight with them on two occasions at Portishead.

John Glover was demobbed in the middle of 1958, and returned to East Leake, near Nottingham, to where his family had moved from Leeds. He kept contact initially and was at the weddings of both Don and Anne and of Joyce and me. Sometime in the earliest days of the motorway system, when the M1 stopped at Rugby, we all piled into cars and descended upon him en masse at East Leake, spending an enjoyable few hours in Nottingham with him and his girlfriend Ann. To the best of my knowledge, he eventually went to New Zealand, and regrettably is no longer in contact.

Brian 'Mitch' Mickels had another year of service to get through after leaving Truleigh Hill early in 1958. His spells at Neatishead and Group Headquarters at Stanmore were not quite the same thing. After demob he went back to the business of printing machinery sales that he was in before service, eventually setting up his own operation. This was however after a spell in Australia in the mid sixties. He married Monica in 1972, and lives in Warlingham in Surrey. Our first major re-union was at their home in 1977.

Don Allwright was the last to leave the RAF, in August 1959, having signed for a three-year term. After Truleigh, Don had spells at Wartling, St. Margaret's and way up on the East Coast at Spurn Head, as well as a stint at Stanmore. Don married Anne within three months of demob, with Joyce as one of the bridesmaids. He is the only one of us still working and has stayed close to his woodworking roots throughout, becoming a partner in a shop-fitting business before taking it over. He continued to play cricket for many years, and is still involved in sailing. We were at each others 40th wedding celebrations, and really should see more of each other since they live a mere six miles away at Lancing. Perhaps we will if he eventually retires one day.

For my part, I am enjoying retirement. Living on the edge of the fantastic South Downs, I would like to spend more time running, but various parts of the body are close to going on permanent strike in protest at many years of misuse. For those who have had the stamina to read through the athletics sections, I am still at it, but only just. I made progress only as far as 1963, finishing with times of 4mins 22.7secs, 14mins 46secs and 31mins 3secs, for one, three and six miles. It has been all downhill since then. Since my first race at school in 1950, I have taken part in nearly eight hundred races and have run a total of almost thirty thousand miles, in seventeen different makes of running shoe, in all but six of the old-style English counties. I was pleased to see my first club at Welwyn make considerable progress, but transferred to Brighton as my main club on settling in Sussex.

I am only very occasionally involved in club athletics nowadays, but in the sixties and seventies I was, at different times, coach, team manager, timekeeper, and statistician among other things. In the early days of Radio Brighton, I even did some commentaries and took part in a regular Saturday evening sports programme, hosted on occasions by a very young Des Lynam.

After spending so much time in the past while writing this story, I have experienced the urge to revisit some of the locations. However I have no desire to visit Cardington, which only occupied one week of my service time, and I have mixed feelings about West Kirby. Until I embarked upon the task of committing my own memories to print, I had no idea of the numbers of National Servicemen who were doing the same thing. Most, however, seem to be just short recollections of one particular station. It is quite understandable that the strongest memories will be of 'square bashing' since so much happened during that two-month period. What is surprising however is the degree of nostalgic affection with which this period is viewed by those who experienced National Service. There is even a West Kirby Association, with regular reunions, and if everything went to plan at the 2004 event, a commemorative plaque should have been unveiled at the old camp entrance.

The area has been preserved as a public open space, but I will have to think carefully about making a special pilgrimage. It is a long way from the South Coast and dodgy knees from a lifetime of running have made long car journeys a problem. St Margaret's and Sandwich are a different matter, being considerably closer, and a visit to both sites resulted in an enjoyable weekend.

Examination of the map showed that a holiday village and an industrial estate respectively now occupy the former domestic sites.

Telephoned enquiries to St. Margaret's revealed that the holiday village boasted a hotel and health club, in addition to the chalets and caravans. Although there were probably better options in the vicinity, it seemed in keeping with the project in general to spend a night on the actual campsite, so Joyce and I made a one night booking at the hotel.

On our arrival in the village, our first visit was to The Hope, which seemed to have changed little since 1956, both inside and out. I half hoped that the chair with the 'Devil's Corner' inscription would still be in the bar, and that someone could confirm if it did indeed relate to Sergeant Dusty Miller. Nearly fifty years on, perhaps this was wishful thinking. Mind you it would not have looked out of place. I tentatively approached a group seated at the bar, who looked to be permanent fixtures, but although they all proved to be patrons of very long standing, none could remember the chair. One however said that his father had worked on the camp and that he remembered going to the cinema there as a child. His status as a pub fixture was confirmed at 11.30 the following morning, when I encountered him on his way to reclaim his seat at the bar.

I had been informed, when making the hotel booking, that the original guardroom was still standing and in use as a store, but there was no evidence of this as we drove in to what I remember as the entrance in 1956. At the location where the guardroom would have been was a timber clad shop and a launderette. Further investigation, and some help from a young shop assistant, revealed a stone structure at the back of the launderette and to the side of the shop. It appeared that both buildings had been built on to the old guardroom. Entry through the launderette took me into several rooms and a toilet, all with a distinct nineteen fifties RAF feel about it.

The hotel room was adequate, but we were not too impressed with the eating facilities. Our visit was in May. The restaurant pictured in the brochure was not yet open for the summer season. This led us to a compromise, which added to the general nostalgia of the occasion. Two miles down the road was The Swingate Hotel, in the shadow of the famous radar towers, where we had an enjoyable evening meal and returned next morning for breakfast. This meant that I had actually slept on the former site of RAF St. Margaret's and had my meals as near as possible to the site where I commenced my Radar Operating career.

Two items were on the agenda for the following morning: to search for the underground site, or what might be left of it, and to test the walk back up the hill from the Green Man pub on the beach. The pub is still there, but somewhere along the line since 1956, it has succumbed to the regrettable trend to tinker with old established pub names, and it is now The Coastguard. From the beach, the road climbs for a couple of hundred yards before reaching the bottom of the steps. One hundred and ninety one steps, through a wooded area later, the path continues on uphill for perhaps another two hundred yards, a total climb of close to 250 feet. I found going down harder than going up. Dodgy knees do not take too kindly to tricky descents, as I have found to my cost on other occasions. Perhaps we should have visited the pub first and sung a few rude songs on the way.

Unlike Truleigh Hill, the underground workings at St. Margaret's had been sealed off many years earlier, but we had a pleasant walk on the countryside above the old operations rooms, which is now part of the Bockhill Farm National Trust area. The house close to the corner of the area, although considerably modernised, has the unmistakable RAF radar guardroom shape and design. It is most definitely the place where I spent the first part of my guard duty before spending the night alone 'down the hole'.

I enjoyed being back at St Margaret's. The cliff-top area where I walked and ran on many occasions all those years ago looked inviting. I am sure that I will be back there fairly soon.

During this weekend we also paid a visit to Sandwich, and as I drove through the ancient tollhouse, over the bridge and onto the Ramsgate road, I knew that I was in the correct area. Shortly after the bridge, a right turn took us down the approach road to the industrial estate, where not only was the old RAF entrance barrier in the same position, but so too was a sorry-looking original guardroom, set at an angle just inside the gate. It looked to be still in use, though probably not as a café despite the large letters on the side of the building. Quite a few more buildings of obvious RAF Sandwich vintage appeared as we drove around the estate, some in use but many others in varying states of disrepair. In contrast, the married quarters, all now private housing, looked in very good condition indeed.

Sandwich town looked much as I remember it, and the camp, though now in different use, looked familiar though a little run down. There was nothing old fashioned or run down about the sight that confronted us shortly after turning out of the industrial estate. If that particular estate looked in need of an injection of cash, there was certainly no financial shortage in evidence as we drove through the massive Pfizer complex that lined both sides of the road, with impressive covered walkways at high level linking the two sides. Either way, between them, they should be doing a power of good for the employment situation in that part of Kent.

At some stage I will probably also revisit Barkway. It is not much more than 100 miles away, and could easily be accommodated within a day trip.

As I have mentioned at the start of the Truleigh Hill chapter, finding information relating to the domestic site is very hard work indeed. I am treating this as a totally separate project and am very slowly gathering photographs and other material from former airmen, old issues of local papers and even memories of local residents. The last airmen left the site in the latter part of 1958, and the camp remained empty until demolition in 1964. I have notes written in 1967, which record that 'council flats are beginning to appear on the hallowed area formerly occupied by billet 19B'. For a period in 1959-60 I lived very close to the camp, and really should have been a bit more on the ball and monitored developments more closely. Today, among the council properties that now fill the whole site, there is absolutely no trace whatsoever of evidence that the RAF once occupied this small corner of Shoreham.

The radar site on Truleigh Hill is a different matter. The guardroom, looking in reasonable shape considering forty-plus years of neglect, still sits in its original position in the middle of the field. Underneath it, the tunnel and rooms are still there, and not sealed off as at St. Margaret's. The site passed into public ownership in 1965 and has had several uses since. I go along that part of the South Downs Way very frequently, either running, walking or cycling, and obviously had noted the guardroom and the remains of various other radar structures. The information regarding the underground area comes courtesy of Squadron Leader Howard Toon, who has done an amazing amount of research, culminating in an excellent web-site containing masses of technical radar information, and many pictures of the underground site as it was in 1998. I have never been 'down the hole' at Truleigh, my entire fifteen months being spent on the above ground GEE system. My knowledge of the operation comes from my involvement in the similar set-up at St. Margaret's.

Much has been written concerning the overall value to the nation of the thirteen years of National Service. That additions to the regular force were necessary during several periods of conflict is not a matter for dispute. Those who served part of their two years in Korea or Malaya or one of the other trouble spots in the dozen years or so after the war will view National Service in a rather different light to those who spent the time on small radar stations in the UK.

But the thirteen years of national service did cost the country a lot. The financial implications of excavating, building and equipping a large number of radar sites around the coast for, in some cases, a period of no more than five years of operation is difficult to imagine. To this can be added the cost of building domestic sites and the feeding, clothing and paying of the operatives. This is just one area of expense for just one of the three forces.

National Service meant many things to many different people. I was very fortunate. Although I did not get the hoped-for opportunity to serve at an overseas posting, I managed to avoid the large impersonal and highly disciplined camps, of which there were many in this country. All in all, the whole exercise of National Service for me had more plus points than minus ones.

Initially it gave me an escape from a highly unsatisfactory home and work situation, placing me in an acceptable environment where we all faced the same problems on a level playing field. It gave me two valuable years in which to prepare to make my own way in the adult world, and it gave me an additional reason for doing so. It also gave me comradeship and memories, and I have enjoyed writing about it. I hope that you have enjoyed reading about it.

~ END ~

Postscript

Since completing the book I have spent a great deal of time researching the history of the Truleigh Hill camp and radar operation. I have also made several attempts to locate some of the key characters mentioned in the book with whom I have had no contact for nearly 50 years.

The main success story in this respect was the discovery of drill instructor Colin 'Geordie' Newton who figures prominently throughout the West Kirby chapter. With the help of Channel 4 Servicepals, the National Service (RAF) Association's extensive membership lists and Charles Sutton, who served with him in Cyprus, he was located just before publication date.

He told me that he had been a drill instructor for ten years, during which time we calculated that he must have scared the hell out of nearly 6,000 recruits! After the discontinuation of National Service he became an RAF policeman. He served a total of 24 years, finishing with the rank of Flight Sergeant and earning the British Empire Medal in the process. Much to my relief, he gave the West Kirby chapter his approval and supplied three of the photographs that appear in this book.

As part of my Truleigh Hill research I have so far found 55 ex-Truleigh personnel. With photographs supplied by them and other items from record offices at Kew and Chichester I was able to stage an exhibition and reunion in the Marlipins Museum in Shoreham which was attended by 34 of them. I was particularly pleased to have found the fourth member of the central room of billet 19B John Loft, the clove-drop consuming champion from East Anglia. John is still living close to his roots at the very top end of Norfolk. He had no hesitation in driving the 500+ miles return trip to Shoreham just for the day.

Equally satisfying was the discovery of Stokoe (Brian Stokes) a mere 20 miles away at Seaford. He cannot remember being found on his back in a ditch at the side of Kingston Lane, but doesn't in any way discount the possibility of it happening!

Unfortunately, not all of my researches ended with happy news. Whilst looking for former St. Margaret's and Truleigh Hill colleague John Saddleton, I came across a Saddleton family history web-site which led me to his brother George. From George I learned the sad news that John had died from a heart attack at the age of 46. He was married with two daughters.

There is a brief mention in the book of Jock Jackson, the No. 90 Group 3 miles champion in 1956. From Ray Spiers, a former colleague of his at RAF Chigwell, I learned that he continued to run for many years but sadly lost his life in 1988 when he was run over and killed while out on a training run.

Two officers encountered at St. Margaret's achieved a degree of fame. Pilot Officer Joan Hopkins, the pleasant young officer in charge of my first radar watch, became the first WRAF officer to take charge of an operational station. As Group Captain Hopkins she became C/O of 500-strong RAF Neatishead in 1982, before retiring as an Air Commodore. The final discovery came from *The Times* obituary of eminent judge James Chadwin, QC, best known for his defence of Peter Sutcliffe, the Yorkshire Ripper. Mention of his earlier career as education officer at RAF Sandwich meant that this was the same Flt/Lt Jim Chadwin who occasionally requested my presence in the Sandwich athletics team.

Digging about in RAF history, particularly on the Internet, can be very time consuming. There are so many web-sites relating to individual stations, or radar in general, that it is very easy to become distracted from the original search. But research goes on. In the Truleigh Hill chapter I expressed surprise at the fact that there was no information in the local libraries relating to a radar operation in Shoreham that ran from 1940 to 1958. In time, this situation will be rectified. I have accumulated sufficient information relating to the post-war period, but wartime material is hard to come by. Meanwhile, there is a permanent display of RAF Truleigh Hill material in the Marlipins Museum in Shoreham which is open between May and October for any interested former airmen, or others, who happen to be in the area.

Six months before call-up. Getting ready for a night on the town at Exmouth 1955.

Back: Tony Dean, Me, Reg Bignell. Centre: Arthur Wood, Graham Haworth, Barry Chipperfield. Front: Tom Ward.

Three months before call-up. Discussing athletics training with local and national heroes at Ludwick House Boys' Club dinner 1955. Top Hertfordshire runner R.W'Digger' Hills in centre, World record-holder Chris Chataway on right.

Fatigues gear, West Kirby 1956.

*Stan Todd, Alan Tapson and I proudly
show off new uniforms at West Kirby.*

Derek Henry, before the RAF barbers at Cardington got to him.

Derek, with hair almost recovered at St. Margaret's later in 1956. Note the Centrimetric Early Warning radar rotating aerial on cliff-top in background.

Entrance to former RAF St. Margaret's in 2004. Shop and laundrette to left of picture have been built onto original guardroom, which has survived intact.

The Hope Inn, St. Margaret's at Cliffe in 2004. Not looking a great deal different, inside and out, from Sergeant Dusty's days half a century earlier.

The famous wartime Chain Home transmitter towers at Swingate, close to Dover Castle, in 2004. My first radar experience was here in rather more peaceful times. The operation closed down during my time there. It is possible that I was on the last ever watch.

Aerial photo of RAF Truleigh Hill domestic site taken after closure of camp in 1958. (West Sussex Records Office)

From top: Pete Mawer, John Saddleton, Dave Glyde, Sheff, Me.

Don Allwright & Brian Mickels (Mitch) on dustbin. Ken Davies, Sheff and Brian Liddington in doorway. Me on step with Ken Smith.

Ken, Don and I being generally stupid!

Shoreham Beach 1957. Don, Taffy Young and Sheff standing. Dave Glyde and John Glover sitting.

With Sheff on Palace Pier, Brighton.

The Baron (John Sapwell) heading for cricket at Buckingham Park.

Leading Carroll (Southgate) and Courtman (Chelmsford) in Chingford Relay 1957.

Start of Brighton Boxing Day race 1957, spread across London Road in front of the Co-Op. Note the trolley-bus lines above. (Evening Argus)

First reunion at Mitch's house in 1977. Standing: The Baron and Mitch.
Seated: Me, Sheff and Don.

Same lot in 1985 at the Baronial residence.

Wives in 1985. Jean Sapwell, Jean Shefford, Anne Allwright and Monica Mickels. Joyce standing behind.

Get-together 1994. Should all be recognisable by now.

$\mathcal{P}rogramme$

For the No. 11 GROUP
R.A.F. and W.R.A.F.

Inter-Station and Individual
Athletic Championships
1957

at the

R.A.F. STADIUM, UXBRIDGE
(by permission of the R.A.F. Sports Board)

on

WEDNESDAY, 12th June, 1957

at 10.30 and 14.30 hours

PRICE 6d.

THREE MILES—R.A.F.

Record Holder: Cpl. RANGER (Tangmere), 14m. 25·2s. 1954.

9 S.A.C. Ward	... Bawdsey	89 S.A.C. Clark	... Sopley
23 S.A.C. Rushbrook	... Biggin Hill	99 S.A.C. Campbell	Stanmore Park
32 S.A.C. Kimberley ...	... Box	120 S.A.C. Curtis	... Tangmere
51 A.C. Evans...	... Duxford	123 S.A.C. Taylor	... Wartling
60 Cpl. Coles ...	... Hope Cove	140 S.A.C. Ganson	... Wattisham
68 Sgt. Clark ...	... Odiham	155 A.C. Chesson	West Malling
82 S.A.C. Stainer	... Sandwich		

1st....99.....2nd..123....3rd................4th.............5th.............6th.............

R CAMPBELL   R TAYLOR   Time.................

TIME   TIME   15

15.00   15.40.

No. 90 (SIGNALS) GROUP
ROYAL AIR FORCE
Individual Athletic Championships.

1957 ATHLETIC R.A.F. & CHAMPIONSHIPS W.R.A.F.

HENLOW WEDNESDAY 19th JUNE, 1957 at 14:15 hrs.

By permission of
GROUP CAPTAIN D. W. SMYTHE,
Officer Commanding
ROYAL AIR FORCE HENLOW.

14.45   6.   3 MILES
(Holder: SAC. Jackson – R.A.F. Chigwell – 15m. 29.8 secs)
1st SAC. TAYLOR... 2nd SAC. EWING... 3rd SAC. JACKSON
UNIT TRIMLEIGH HILL UNIT STANBRIDGE UNIT CHIGWELL
WINNING TIME... 15m. 33s

Event No. 45   **15.10 hours**
THREE MILES (Final)

For statuette presented by A.O.C.-in-C., Officers and Airmen of Coastal Command

Holder: A.C. C. E. FRENCH (F.C.)
British Record: C. J. CHATTAWAY, 13 mins. 23·2 secs., 1955
Inter-Services Record: L.A.C. G. D. IBBOTSON, R.A.F., 13 mins. 52·8 secs., 1955
R.A.F. Record: L.A.C. G. D. IBBOTSON (**), 13 mins. 50·8 secs., 1955

623 Cpl. Palmer, H. C. (C) (F.T.C.)	703 Fg/Off. C. G. H. Pierce (C.C.)
629 S.A.C. Hurst, T. J. ... (F.T.C.)	238 A.C. Langridge, R. (*) (T.T.C.)
335 L.A.C. Taylor, D. G.	204 Fg/Off. A. J. Wood ... (T.T.C.)
(C) ... ... (M.C.)	136 S.A.C. French, C. E.... (F.C.)
342 A.C. Hawes, J. ... (M.C.)	132 S.A.C. Campbell, R. ... (F.C.)
436 L.A.C. Moody, M. J.... (B.C.)	921 S.A.C. Taylor, R. F. (C) (90 G.)
411 Sgt. Carnelley, M. B.... (B.C.)	914 S.A.C. Ewing, G. L. ... (90 G.)
819 S.A.C. Berry, A. (C)... (T.C.)	524 L.A.C. Batty, R. C. (C) (H.C.)
822 L.A.C. Bratt, J. R. ... (T.C.)	529 L.A.C. Myers, F. C. ... (H.C.)
712 Cpl. Shearer, W. (C) ... (C.C.)	206 Plt/Off. M. J. Reeve... (Ind.)

Reserves: 133 206 343 432 830

1st .. 136 FRENCH ^CE .. 2nd .. 204 WOOD ^AJ .. 3rd .. 244 RIGBY W.

Time .. 14m 10s .. Time .. 14m 28s .. Time .. 14m 42s

4th...................... 5th...................... 6th......................

Time .... Time .... Time .... FAVOURITES
LANGRIDGE
10h. = 921 TAYLOR ^RF 15m 33s   & REEVE DID
NOT FINISH.

Three miles final. RAF Athletics Championships 1957.

No. 90 (SIGNALS) GROUP

Team Manager: SQUADRON LEADER H. C. MOLYNEUX, O.B.E., R.E.U. Henlow

Team Captain: W.O. MANN, D., R.E.U. Henlow

901 Fg/Off. I. S. M. PAUL, R.I.U., Malvern
902 Fg/Off. D. WRIGHT, R.E.U., Henlow
903 W.O. MANN, D., R.E.U., Henlow
904 F/Sgt. COWIE, A., Bishopbriggs
905 F/Sgt. PERKINS, C. A., C.S.E., Watton
906 F/Sgt. ROBERTS, R. V., C.S.E., Watton
907 Cpl. ALDRED, D. H., C.S.E., Watton
908 Cpl. BELCHER, F. D., Chigwell
909 Cpl. SAPWELL, J. W., Truleigh Hill
910 Cpl. WHITEHOUSE, R. J., R.E.U., Henlow
911 J/Tech. LEWIN, D. P., Stanbridge
912 J/Tech. ROE, D. G., Chigwell
913 S.A.C. BENN, J., Chigwell
914 S.A.C. EWING, G. L., Stanbridge
915 S.A.C. GOLDSTEIN, A. A., R.E.U., Henlow
916 S.A.C. GRIGGS, G. R., Chigwell
917 S.A.C. HENDERSON, G., R.E.U., Henlow

918 S.A.C. HUGHES, D., Bishopbriggs
919 S.A.C. MCKECHIE, T., Newmarket
920 S.A.C. SANDERS. N. G., C.S.E., Watton
921 S.A.C. TAYLOR, R. F., Truleigh Hill
922 S.A.C. THOMSON, J., Haydock
923 S.A.C. WATKINS, D., Chigwell
924 L.A.C. EDWARDS, M., Chigwell
925 L.A.C. GOOD, J. D., R.E.U., Henlow
926 L.A.C. HAITH, B. A., Stanbridge
927 L.A.C. MARSHAM, I. A., Chigwell
928 L.A.C. NIMMO, J. G., Chigwell
929 L.A.C. PITTOCK, M., Stanbridge
930 L.A.C. RICHARDS, C., Newmarket
931 A.C. FROMANT, D. A., Pucklechurch
932 A.C. LEWIS, J., Wythall
933 A.C. ROBERTS, N., Stanbridge

Tug-of-War: R.E.U., HENLOW. Coach: CPL. MCINTYRE, R.

J/Tech. ROBERTS, W.
S.A.C. BIRCH, J.
S.A.C. GALLACHER, J.
S.A.C. GARDINER, R.
S.A.C. GUILOR

S.A.C. RAYNOR, R.
S.A.C. ROWNTREE, J.
S.A.C. TODD, B.
S.A.C. WALLACE, W.
L.A.C. PINSON, P.

W.R.A.F.

Team Manager: CPL. BROOKS, J. C. W., Stanbridge

Team Captain: CPL. PEARSON, J. M., Stanbridge

951 Cpl. PEARSON, J. M., Stanbridge
952 Cpl. BROOKS, J. C. W., Stanbridge
953 Cpl. BUSHELL, C., Medmenham
954 Cpl. CORKHILL, V., Haydock
955 S.A.C.W. CORELESS, J. E., Haydock

956 S.A.C.W. HARRISON, P. A., Stanbridge
957 S.A.C.W. WHELAN, P. N. E., Gloucester
958 L.A.C.W. KEYHOE, C., Haydock
959 A.C.W. DRYLAND, J. A., Stanbridge

No.90(Signals) Group team for 1957 RAF Championships.

ROYAL AIR FORCE

R.A.F. FORM 1394.
(Revised December, 1951.)
(For issue only to National
Service Airmen and Airwomen
not on regular engagements).

BRIEF STATEMENT OF SERVICE AND CERTIFICATE ON DISCHARGE

1. Surname _TAYLOR R.F._   Official No. _2782765_
   Christian Names _ROY FREDERICK_   Rank on Discharge _SAC._
2. Period of whole-time service. From _9.1.56_   To _8.2.58_
3. Trade in civil life _Toolmaker_   4. R.A.F. trade on entry _U.T. Rad. Op._
5. Details of any R.A.F. trade training _Basic Grade Training_
6. R.A.F. trade on discharge and brief description of duties. (vide A.M. Pamphlet 51.)
   RADAR OPERATOR (GEE):
   Complete knowledge of the principles of GEE radar systems.

7. Assessments of Conduct, Proficiency and Personal Qualities during service :—

	Exemplary	Very Good	Good	Fairly Good	Poor
(a) Conduct	EX				
	Exceptional	Very Good	Good	Fairly Good	Poor
(b) Ability as tradesman/aircrew* *Delete as inapplicable		VG			
(c) Ability as supervisor in his trade (Applicable to N.C.O.s only)			—		
(d) Personal Qualities :—					
(i) Leadership			Gd		
(ii) Co-operation			Gd		
(iii) Bearing (to be assessed "Very Smart," "Smart," or "Untidy")				Smart	

8. Medals, Clasps, Decorations, Mentions in Despatches, etc.
9. Reason for Discharge _Completion of whole-time National Service_
10. REMARKS. (This section to be used only to amplify Assessments, trade qualifications, etc., where necessary.)
    A cheerful & Capable Airman

11. DESCRIPTION ON DISCHARGE
    Height _5_ ft. _2_ ins.   Colour of Hair _Brown_
    Complexion _Fresh_   Marks or Scars
    Colour of Eyes _Hazel_   _NIL_
12. National Service airmen are liable to undergo part-time service—See notice overleaf.

STATION H.Q.
-7 JAN 1958
R.A.F. MEDMENHAM

Signed _____
Commanding   **R.A.F. MEDMENHAM**   Rank _Wg. Cdr._

Signature of Airman/Airwoman _R.F.Taylor._

(*1995—1403) Wt. 38040—3005 3,600 Pads 3/52 T.S. 839

The End!